FROM ROBE TO ROBE

FROM ROBE TO ROBE

A Lesbian's Spiritual Journey

MARTHA E. BELLINGER.

TRAFFORD PUBLISHING

BLOOMINGTON, IN

To our God who gave me the spiritual journey which resulted in this book as well as the courage to write it, and to all gay, lesbian, bisexual and trans-gender people who have been wandering the desert for too long and deserve to enter the promised land.

Order this book online at www.trafford.com
or email orders@trafford.com

Most Trafford titles are also available at major online book retailers.

Printed in Victoria, BC, Canada.

ISBN: 978-1-4269-3348-6 (sc)

ISBN: 978-1-4269-3349-3 (hc)

ISBN: 978-1-4269-3350-9 (e-book)

Library of Congress Control Number: 2010907743

Our mission is to efficiently provide the world's finest, most comprehensive book publishing service, enabling every author to experience success. To find out how to publish your book, your way, and have it available worldwide, visit us online at www.trafford.com

Trafford rev. 7/5/2010

 www.trafford.com

North America & international
toll-free: 1 888 232 4444 (USA & Canada)
phone: 250 383 6864 ♦ fax: 812 355 4082

"For now we see in a mirror dimly, but then face to face. Now I know in part; then I shall understand fully, even as I have been fully understood."

I Corinthians 13:12

"He has showed you, O man, what is good. And what does the Lord require of you? To act justly and to love mercy and to walk humbly with your God."

Micah 6:8

"And we know that in all things God works for the good of those who love him, who have been called according to his purpose."

Romans 8:28

"Four things belong to a judge; to hear courteously, to answer wisely, to consider soberly, and to decide impartially.

Socrates

Preface

It took a long time to have enough faith in God to overcome my fears of rejection and write this book. It should be said straight off that several individuals who mean a great deal to me in this life, as well as most of the greater Christian church, find it difficult, if not impossible, to understand how a woman could call herself a lesbian and a Christian. I call myself a Christian because the life and teachings of Jesus fully embrace my aspirations in living a spiritual life. However, I have high regard for other religious paths, most especially Judaism and Buddhism. I believe God comes to individuals in many different ways, and if the "religion" which is practiced does not denigrate particular races, genders, or sexual orientations, it is a religion I can respect, and its followers, people with whom I can openly dialogue about our meaning and purpose in this world.

I do see a clear distinction between being spiritual and being religious. I believe being spiritual means a genuine search for the presence of God in one's life, while being religious means pursuing this search through a set of organized principles which most often results in the affiliation with a particular institution promoting these principles. I believe one can be spiritual without the help of organized religion, and I believe one can be spiritual and can be part of a religious organization. However, I question the mission of any organized religion which seeks to confine an individual's spiritual search through a rigid set of precepts and principles.

Christian fundamentalists as well as many feminists would no doubt agree on this point - the terms lesbian and Christian appear to be mutually exclusive. Consequently, to call oneself just that - a lesbian Christian - is to subject oneself to ridicule by both sides of the moral debate on the acceptability of homosexuality within our society, and within Christ's church.

About the time I decided to begin this book for my own coming out process, as well as for all my gay brothers and lesbian sisters who need to have some semblance of hope for a place within Christ's church, I happened to run across this quote from a book written by the great scientist, philosopher and spiritual teacher, Emmett Fox: "The soul's integrity is the one and only thing that matters . . . . And so Jesus in his teaching is almost exclusively concerned in impressing us with the overwhelming fact of its importance, and with instructing us on how we are to accomplish it. He insists that positively no sacrifice can be too great to insure the integrity of one's soul. Anything, anything that stands in the way of that, must be given up. Cost what it will, involve what it may, the integrity of the soul must be preserved; for all other things - conduct, health, prosperity - life itself - follow upon that."

Suddenly writing this book also became a matter of the very integrity of my soul. "Cost what it will, involve what it may," I must let the world know, that my heart has always held the abiding belief that I am a good part of God's creation - that God loves and affirms me as I am. While there is plenty of room for spiritual improvement in my life, I've come to understand any deficits I might have in this regard have nothing whatsoever to do with my sexual orientation.

An older straight couple who invited me to their home for dinner one evening several years ago, commented after hearing my life story, that they were surprised I still believed in God after my many experiences of prejudice, rejection, and heartbreak. No one had ever said that to me before, and it made me think about how fortunate I was to have hung onto God's love through all the pain in my life.

Somehow I learned in my last year of college, when I made a conscious choice for the first time to follow Christ's teachings, that this was not a way of comfort or ease - that there might be peace at the end of the journey but that there would be plenty of suffering and adversity before my life was perfected. The theology of suffering, which was popular during my years in college and seminary, reinforced this belief. I am aware that most people operate under the false assumption that a belief in God makes life easier to live. But in a very real sense, a belief in God complicates living because one is then faced with living the questions - trying to understand why God allows hate when God is supposed to be about love; why God tolerates human suffering in any form when God is omnipotent. I don't have pat answers for these enigmas. I only believe, as one theologian said long ago, that God isn't going to fix anything that we can fix ourselves, and somehow I have felt God's love in the midst of the darkest periods of my life. This is my experience of grace - this is my faith.

Life is certainly a puzzle, and my own life experience speaks volumes about paradox, irony, and mystery. Just when I thought I had the purpose and meaning of my life all figured out, life took such a sudden, new direction, that all my preconceived notions were dashed upon the rocks of my arrogance. I Corinthians 13:12 says it all. We only know a small part of what our life is all about. We see through a mirror dimly. If we seek understanding by allowing ourselves to experience life instead of trying to constantly control and will its direction, we gain more awareness of our purpose.

It is my hope in letting go of my own fears of rejection, and sharing my life story with you, that you will understand more clearly how God's grace and acceptance does extend to those of us who are gay or lesbian. If just one soul can be lifted by this story, God's purpose has been served.

Throughout this book I will use the terms gay, lesbian, bisexual and trans-gender, interchangeably, all to reflect the common designation used for our community as the LGBT community. If the LGBT terminology is not used each time I refer to our community it is not to exclude anyone of my brothers or sisters who fit one of these designations, but for purposes of brevity only.

I have chosen not to use the real name of my first partner but rather refer to her by a nickname I gave to her when she once expressed the fact she hated her first name. I suggested to her in 1973 a very proper and up-scale designation of Victoria. She signed her letters to me with this name. I have maintained her anonymity, for you will see she was very uncomfortable being completely out when "married" to me. She died tragically years after leaving our relationship, but I think it important to respect her privacy and that of her remaining family. I have never believed in "outing" people for we each have to make our own decision in that regard.

ACKNOWLEDGMENTS

I wish to thank Talene Mannahan for her excellent proofreading and editing services performed in the development of this book. Dennis Lloyd, a long-time friend and excellent artist, was the individual who did the outstanding design for the front cover of this book. I thank my spouse, Pam, for her assistance in some of the technical aspects of physically generating the text and for her constant encouragement in my writing endeavors.

CONTENTS

CHAPTER ONE

From Tomboy To Preacher

I was born on a dairy farm in Upstate New York on March 1, 1950. Life on the farm was in many respects idyllic - a Norman Rockwell kind of existence. It was a less complicated time in our nation's history in some respects. The importance of the proverbial nuclear family was not debated, it just was. We were a family of five. It might have been a tad more perfect if one of the three daughters had been a son, but I was the last attempt at that feat, and my parents eventually had to settle for a tomboy. I don't actually remember my parents bemoaning the fact that they had no son, however, and I once remember my father reciting the phrase in support of his happiness with three daughters that "a son was a son until he took a wife, but a daughter was a daughter for the rest of her life."

I am eternally grateful for what my parents gave me in terms of core values. My parents believed in hard work, fidelity in relationships, and when it came to matters of race, my parents were among the few in conservative Upstate New York who possessed not a prejudiced bone in their bodies. When we eventually moved off the dairy farm when I was

12 years old, we lived in a small city which had but one African American church. My father, a lay leader in the United Methodist Church, was asked to preach in this African Methodist Episcopal church on more than one occasion and it was my mother who taught the pastor's wife of that church how to play the piano. In our own church, we had but one African American family, which my parents befriended and they did the best they could to console this family when they lost their only son in the Vietnam War on Christmas Eve 1968.

My parents, until their own infirmities from old age, always visited the sick, helped the poor, and remained true to their convictions. My parents were honest to a fault, and when they said they were going to do something for you, you could count on it. When they were still in their eighties, they helped man the local food pantry once a week for an ecumenical urban mission where my father had earlier served as a founding member and eventual chairman of its board years before. I hope I honor them with similar characteristics in my relationships with others.

As I recall my childhood on the farm, I realize I was not the average little girl who was proud of her patent leather shoes and frilly dresses. While my older sisters were preoccupied with making the cheerleading squad and laboriously rolling up their hair each night on curlers, I was content to be in the barn helping my father tend our dairy cows, and at about age ten, I began spending endless hours on our tractor raking hay for baling in the good old summertime. I usually preferred to be outside of the house by myself, and I would literally stand on a tree stump in our back yard giving speeches on various topics. It was the humble beginnings of an affinity for public speaking I would utilize at college rallies, in the pulpit, from the bench, teaching in the law classroom and addressing many organizations concerned about children's rights and the law in these later years of my life.

When I did have playmates from the nearby village or farms, it was always a boy. We played endless games of baseball for which I became known as the most accomplished player in my age group. Few boys could bat better or throw a ball farther than I. My father forced my sisters to play many games of softball with me when we lived on the farm and Dad often exclaimed, "Look at the wing on that girl," referring to my throwing ability. I was a husky, but fit, young farm girl and when I made contact with a softball, it went places! I was always running, climbing, exploring the world around me. I was a big girl, the tallest student in my class through sixth grade save for one boy who would grow to be nearly six feet, four inches in adult life. Staying inside and tending dolls with tea parties held no interest.

At the same time I became absolutely fascinated with learning and reading. At this early age I knew I wanted to work toward some career in public service and saw no limitation to this goal on the basis that I was a girl! As I look back on those early years, I clearly see I was different from most of my female peers - our aspirations and activities were disparate. Was this all due to my sexual orientation of which I was so blissfully ignorant at that time? Certainly that factor informed the difference to some extent. It has been my experience that many lesbian women are often blessed with an unusually well developed sense of confidence and assertiveness. These attributes are often perceived offensively by much of society, unfortunately. I'm sure that much of this confidence in lesbians is attributable to the lesbian child's innate sense that she need not please boys to be happy or successful. Perhaps now, as cultural expectations for little boys and girls have slowly changed for the better, straight girls are also learning what many lesbian girls have always intuited - that females are every bit as capable and are equally valuable members of society as their male counterparts.

I suppose I had an early inclination as to my sexual orientation in high school but kept it quite buried. I had a very dear friend in high school with whom I felt a very special bond. There were never any intimacies shared between us, but for much of these adolescent years we were inseparable. We played countless games of tennis and fancied ourselves as aspiring Billie Jean Kings. How ironic that in our mid-twenties my friend and I would come out to one another as lesbians, and we would later learn our childhood idol was also "one of us."

Nevertheless I dated boys throughout high school, went to my senior prom, and had my heart broken at least once by the one boy who really interested me - a football player and popular member of our class. Immediately following graduation I became heavily involved with another young man with whom I had a whirlwind summer romance. During the fall semester of my freshman year at college I even contemplated marrying him. He seemed different from several boys I had dated up to that time. He never pressured me into having sex with him more than once. When I said no, largely because it felt uncomfortable and unnatural to me, he respected my "no" and continued to want our relationship despite my unwillingness "to do it." However, as I moved further into my freshman year and we remained physically separated by our respective colleges, my desire to keep up this relationship waned and I eventually told him I wanted to end the relationship.

In the fall of 1968, I went off to Syracuse University. Despite some difficult emotional adjustments my first year at this large cosmopolitan university, I eventually took to the diversity of this academic institution as the proverbial duck takes to water. For the first time I had many Jewish friends and some African American friends. It was that special time in our nation's history, and the campuses of our country, particularly Syracuse University, where there were few fence sitters on the war and peace issue. You were either a "hawk" or a "dove," a "flower child" or a "pig," part of the "Establishment" or part of the "in" crowd. As such,

I did some very admirable things, such as peacefully demonstrate for the end of the Vietnam War, and I did some very dumb things like all young adults of that time were so well known for doing. But we were convinced that we had found the way to truth, and that those on the other side of the fence were mere Neanderthals who were intent on pushing our world toward oblivion.

I must admit that deep down I was a bit uncomfortable with this moral absolution with which everyone seemed so comfortable. Somehow I knew the world wasn't quite this black and white. Yet the lines had been drawn and I knew which side of the line I had to occupy. It was perhaps because of this discomfort with absolutes, line-drawing and near violent demonstrations, that I often found myself serving as a mediator in the midst of campus confrontations. The most moving of those experiences was the prayer I was asked to give on our campus quadrangle at the memorial service for the Kent State students who had been shot by the National Guard in Ohio in May 1970. I don't exactly recall what I said to the 3,000 plus students inside and outside Hendricks Chapel, I just remembered the tragedy we all felt and the obligation to not let these lives pass in vain, or to have as their only memorial, more hatred and violence in the streets. I felt the empowerment of thousands joined together in the name of peace and justice.

In 1997, 27 years after this tragedy at Kent State, I visited that campus for the first time and took several moments to stand by the simple memorial erected to the memory of the dead students. Ironically, it was Memorial Day weekend, and a Vietnam War soldier had attached a letter to the memorial addressed to the fallen students. In the letter he related that on the very day the students were killed on the Kent State campus, his platoon in Viet Nam had been ambushed with several of his comrades having been killed. What was remarkable about this letter was that the soldier bore no ill will any longer toward the demonstrators. He only acknowledged that at that time in our nation's history there were many losses for both sides of the controversy, and it no longer mattered who had been right or wrong about our involvement in the conflict. Death was death, and the death of people barely out of their teens was a tragedy to be mourned no matter where or how it happened. I can only pray that all of us who lived during that time and cared so deeply for our position no matter what it happened to be, could reach this level of understanding and peace this soldier had found.

I remained active in the anti-war movement throughout my time at Syracuse. I became conversant with peaceful demonstration as a way of bringing others attention to the problems of the moment. This perhaps naive understanding of dealing with conflicts even took a humorous overtone on one occasion. I recall my sophomore year serving as president of my dormitory when all our bathroom facilities became inoperable for two days. As we approached our third day with no plumbing repairs, you can imagine that 100 young women were in no mood for compromise. We needed hot showers and a toilet we could flush, and the central administration seemed to be dragging their feet. We could call the health department and report the university, which might take a day or two more to resolve the problems, or we could do something more immediate.

We were next door to the Chancellor's mansion and I decided at 9 p.m. that evening to lead my fellow students up the driveway to the Chancellor's mansion and ask to use the bathroom. So, the fire alarm was pulled, all the coeds poured out of the dormitory, and in bathrobes and curlers, we marched to the door where we were greeted by a somewhat nervous, elderly security guard who wanted to know what we wanted. I told him we needed to use the Chancellor's bathroom facilities since ours had been broken for two days. With a smile on my face, I listened to his frantic car radio call back to the central security office of the university informing them that he had nearly 100 women in nightgowns and bathrobes camped out on the Chancellor's doorstep and he needed reinforcements immediately. Within two hours our plumbing was fixed.

I had learned the art of confrontational politics, but while I have always felt comfortable facing down my adversaries in my professional life, it has never been that easy for me to be confrontational in my personal life. If I had to risk the loss of love from someone I valued, I would do almost anything to avoid the pain of confrontation. How easy it is to create this dichotomy between what we do at work and what we live at home. Overcoming this dichotomy is perhaps what we would have called in the 1960's, self-actualization.

During my freshman year at Syracuse University, I became very aware I was attracted to a woman friend. I never told her I was in love with her, and ended the pain of being "so near, and yet so far away," by moving to a different dormitory mid-year. While I was fascinated and completely in love with this woman, I also suffered tremendous depression. My conservative training told me this was all wrong, and I felt badly about myself for having these forbidden thoughts of wanting to hold her and care for her. I saw the campus psychologist a couple of times but never told him why I was depressed. After the second session this "insightful" man blithely commented that he felt I was "too serious about life" - that "I thought too much," and that I should just "go out and have a good time." That was certainly easier said than done as a lesbian woman in 1968, especially when you didn't yet fully understand what that meant.

Dating was not the main priority for me at Syracuse University. I dated men a good bit my freshman year at SU but after that point in time, any desire to date men was lost to more pressing pursuits of academics and the tumultuous campus politics of the time. To my knowledge, I became the first woman at SU to run for student body president. I lost the election but garnered substantial support, and felt the cause of women in politics at SU had moved forward a significant degree. It is true as other women of my generation have observed that in those times, women in the peace movement and the civil rights movement were largely seen as girls who could fetch and tote coffee, weed, or offer sex to the men of the "movement" who were really seen as the movers and shakers of that generation.

During my last year at Syracuse I experienced a true religious renaissance in my life. It was time for me to decide where I would go from here. I was a political science major somewhat interested in law school. I also had a religion minor, and it was through this religious studies program that I experienced my rebirth as a committed Christian. Curiously the pilgrimage began in a Buddhism course. I was taken with the Buddha's teachings - the middle road - the freeing of the self from desire which prevented an individual from achieving peace and serenity. As I sat in that course the thought kept recurring, "I've heard these themes before," yet this is my first venture into the study of Buddhism.

I decided to take a fresh look at my own religious tradition. I decided to reread the Gospels, the cornerstone of Jesus' teachings. The memory of sitting on my couch in my college apartment reading the Sermon on the Mount and shedding tears from a new understanding of what Jesus was all about will remain fresh in my mind until I leave this life. I had been a star student of the Bible throughout my Sunday school years. I could probably quote more verses than anyone. But that was all meaningless now. The Christian faith was not mine until that moment.

Some 38 years later I understand why the Sermon on the Mount had such a powerful message for me. After my careful study this last decade of spiritual teacher Emmet Fox's book about the true meaning of the Sermon on the Mount and in particular, his discussion of the Beatitudes in particular had a powerful new meaning for me. Being "poor in spirit" for Emmet Fox means emptying ourselves of all menaningless desires of this world and concentrating on our God and God's purpose for our life in serving our fellow human beings. When we do this, we actually become complete, at peace with who we are in this world.

After that experience at Syracuse my senior year, I began to wonder again about how best my life should be spent. I knew I wanted to help people in some way and I had this religious renaissance which I felt was pointing me toward ministry. Although I had also thought about going to law school I was sure God was calling me to what I believed naively to be a "higher calling." Thirty seven years later I realize God had much to teach me about what real ministry entails and that sometimes the church is the last place where true ministry for the world really happens. But in the Fall of 1971 I talked to the Dean of Hendrick's Chapel at Syracuse University. He advised me to apply to Harvard, Yale, Princeton, Union or Chicago for a Master of Divinity program. I visited Princeton that Fall and fell in love with the Princeton campus and community. During Christmas vacation I received an acceptance notice from Princeton indicating they were extending a full scholarship to that institution. I was all set, and my parents could not have been happier that my life appeared to be off in a superior direction.

I credit my alma mater, Syracuse University, with giving me a new world view, a new lease on life. But for this university experience, my tolerance of, and openness to different people and different ideas would have remained measurably constrained by the small town attitudes of my childhood. It was this ability to appreciate alternatives to what had always been that provided the cornerstone of my own acceptance as a capable, socially conscious lesbian woman. While my conservative acquaintances in life might consider Syracuse University the beginning of my downfall, for me, I know it was here I found the value of my talents, first accepted Christ's teachings as my chosen way of life, and discovered my true humanity.

I found a lot more at Princeton Theological Seminary than theology and the fine art of preaching - I found my sexual orientation. After another brief whirlwind romance with a male seminarian, I met a feminist at Princeton who stole my heart for ten and a half years. We would proceed cautiously over a period of months into an intimate relationship. We would move through a sort of courtship for six months before we were brave enough to join our bodies together in an experience of passion and spiritual bonding never before experienced by either of us. Before that first night of intimacy took place, we talked about what it would mean to move into sexual intimacy with one another. It was my partner's struggle more than mine. I had no doubt or guilt any longer about being a lesbian. I knew instinctively that God loved me, and for some reason wanted me to have this particular sexual identity. I knew my partner was a good, kind, and brilliant woman, and that I wanted to spend my life with her. Despite these feelings about her, I waited for her to make the first move toward sexual intimacy.

We had been joined side by side in the fight for women's recognition in the mainline protestant ministry. We had spent numerous evenings talking into the wee hours of the morning about feminist theology, and women's rights. Through this process we came to respect each other's mind and soul. It seemed only natural to consummate this marriage of minds through sexual contact. Some 25 years after this partner chose to leave my life, I still remember her fine mind and spirituality, and I will always treasure those early days in the feminist movement when I found out for sure I was a lesbian in the arms of a tender, spiritually aware woman. That was October 1973 and I was 23 years old.

In a journal entry from 1973, I discussed my first encounter with my beloved Victoria. I share it with you now to help you understand the intensity of my feelings. I wrote:

"There is absolutely no doubt in my mind that this meeting of Victoria was Providential. I had no particular desire to go to the women's meeting at Princeton Seminary tonight, feeling that my head was not in the same place as most of fellow women seminarians. In my mind this patriarchal institution around us was killing us - book by book, lecture by lecture, we were becoming acceptable token women in a profession most certainly meant only for men. The weekend before this meeting, a handful of us went to a women's conference at Union Theological Seminary in Virginia addressing issues of women in ministry. The keynote speaker had been Mary Daly, author of the book "Beyond God the Father." For most of us at that conference our minds had been stretched to new levels thinking about a concept of God that did not confine itself to male imagery.

As I walked home from the meeting this evening, I asked myself, 'Where am I in my life?'. Technically speaking I am in seminary studying for the ministry. Princeton is surely one of those seminaries which worship at the feet of Augustine, Barth and liberation theologians who basically intend liberation for everyone but the fairer sex. No matter now. The point is that God choose this place for me to meet Victoria, and perhaps if we had not both felt so oppressed and angry, by the Ivy League surroundings and all the paternalism it represented, we would have never met but rather passed each other by.

This Victoria has quite a reputation on the campus as being an uncompromising feminist who dared speak out against the absurdity of our existence at this place. She didn't neatly fit into the propriety of the place. Perhaps that is why I never got to know her when I first arrived - I wanted in my first few weeks here to fit in, to climb the ladder of the patriarchy with female finesse.

So here I was at this women's meeting telling my unconvinced female seminarians that they needed to expand their minds about God, and opt out of this overly simplistic idea of God the Father.

I was telling my story of personal mind liberation and across from me sat a lady with the most incredible green eyes you've ever seen. She had on a long black dress - fresh from a play rehearsal - and yes, she had tears rolling down her cheeks. Every time I vented a little bit of my bitterness and anger during that discussion, the lady with green eyes would let another tear roll down her cheek. She then looked at me directly, and for the first time in my life I felt like saying to a woman, 'Hey, where have you been all my life?.'

When the meeting ended my lady in black left the room to get her coat. I wanted to follow her but I was being harangued by a million questions by my fellow women seminarians. My friends were trying to convince me that I had totally flipped out of sacred time. After all, I had been 'progressing' very well here at the seminary before I heard this lady, Mary Daly. Maybe if I just cooled out for a couple days I'd put things back into 'perspective.' Oh why didn't they just shut up. The lady in the black dress had just left the room. Didn't they feel the loss?

Yes, yes, yes, I promised them, I would go out for coffee and discuss this some more but it would be useless. I don't need a cup of coffee, I needed to talk to that woman with those incredible green eyes. What the hell am I saying! I've never talked to myself like this before - I've never felt so intensely about a woman in this way. But hell, Mary Daly says it is all right to think about women - that's all we've got - our thoughts, our hopes for a more woman friendly society, and the collective unconsciousness of our foremothers.

God, it's too good to believe. The lady with the sad green is coming back into the room and she's headed toward me. She says she appreciated what I had to say. That's not important - she said more to me in one glance than a book full of feminist history and theology, sociology or psychology."

So that was my journal entry in 1973 about my meeting Victoria for the first time. It was obvious to me I was head over heels infatuated with this brilliant woman. After we committed to one another and entered an intimate relationship, the meeting of our eyes would always be like that. Every time we climbed into bed, or listened to music together as we frequently did, or went to the movies, or swimming, we would stare at each other in disbelief - the fascination continued with one another. We seemed to connect deeply on every level - spiritual, emotional, intellectual and physical.

During my second year at Princeton, I was given a grant by the seminary to start the first women's center which was meant to educate both men and women about the role of women in the church and ministry. Victoria had been instrumental in pressing the seminary to open this center and I was chosen by the Dean to be that person. So in a humble room of the student center at Princeton I, with incredible help from Victoria, opened the Princeton Theological Seminary Women's Center. We created a library of materials dealing with women's spirituality which we loaned out to all interested students, male and female. We invited special speakers to the seminary to address issues of women's roles in the church and ministry. Victoria and I worked side by side on this project for a year, and at year's end we held a very large three day seminar on "Women and the Church," which was attended by women throughout the Northeast as we featured guest speakers who were leaders in feminist theology.

The Women's Center was not without controversy and I was often accused of being a "man-hater," and other choice words. This hurt me on some level because I thought I was very non-confrontational about these concerns, but starting such a project at a seminary not used to large numbers of women in the classes was sure to bring these criticisms. That is not to say we did not have our supporters even among our fellow male seminarians. In fact one such man became very infatuated with me and asked to date me just at the time I had begun my relationship with Victoria. He had no knowledge of that relationship and was shocked to learn of it but he was not about to "out us" and actually became a good friend to both Victoria and I.

There is no doubt that this intense struggle for equality at Princeton brought Victoria and I together in a very fundamental way. We respected each other's minds and we moved to that same level of trust when it concerned our souls and our bodies. An intimate relationship was inevitable for us.

After we became sexually intimate for the first time, my partner had some momentary regret. She was frightened somewhat that our friendship had taken this turn. While I tried to understand her confusion, I could not fully appreciate this reaction because our physical relationship seemed so natural and beautiful to me. I was experiencing with her a closer emotional bond unlike any other I had experienced in life. I would learn years later that my partner was clearly bisexual, while I was comfortable as a lesbian.

As previously mentioned I have not used my first partner's real name in this book because for the most part she preferred to remain closeted throughout our relationship except for a few close friends, mostly lesbian friends, and we came out to her parents in 1975. When she left me in 1984 to explore the world of men, she made a complete break from me and did not want any contact with me whatsoever. She ended up dying in a car accident with her husband 13 years later. My heart broke again when I learned of her death. I had hoped that one day we could sit down over a cup of tea and thank each other for what we had meant to one another. As she wished to remain in the closet in life, I will respect that right even in death. Somehow I believe she has a whole different understanding of what this period of our lives was all about as she watches from the other side.

As we came to the end of the 1973-1974 academic year at Princeton, I was faced with two dilemmas. My partner was in the class ahead of me and would graduate. How could we stay together with me in school for one more year, and her out? Princeton as a community was not exactly a place where my partner could find employment outside the church. We might have a "marriage" in our eyes, but no married student housing was available to us. We were also very closeted and desirous of escaping the microscope of the seminary community. So I decided we should move on to another larger community where I could finish my theology degree, my partner could find some meaningful employment, and we could have some anonymity living together. Boston University School of Theology became the solution. Given a full scholarship by Boston, and a job as a professor's research assistant, the two of us packed our few worldly belongings into my 1965 Oldsmobile and we drove off to the Bay State.

The other dilemma I faced in the spring of 1974 was whether or not I would be ordained as a deacon in the United Methodist Church. In the United Methodist Church, ordination as a pastor was a two step process. You were first ordained to the status of deacon and permitted to perform all the sacraments, as well as pastor a church. After a year of performing adequately in this role, you could then become an elder of the church, which essentially gave you ecclesiastical voting rights which you did not have as a deacon. I had already deferred this ordination as a deacon after my first year at Princeton, and it was now a moment of decision. I knew my Board of Ministry would clearly look askance at a lesbian minister, and I wondered how God would feel about my inability to assume a prophetic role in this regard. Of course, they had no inkling I was a lesbian. However, I pressed on with ministry plans and went through the ordination in June of 1974, with my partner watching the ceremony.

My time at Boston University School of Theology was somewhat of a respite from the growing conservatism in the mainline churches, which had begun to infect the academic environment of many seminaries in the mid-seventies, despite the population increase of women students in seminary. The academic air of Boston University School of Theology seemed to be more liberal and socially conscious than Princeton. Courses on human sexuality and social ethics at Boston University taught tolerance and understanding toward the homosexual community. I had one openly gay man in many of my classes at Boston University. The city of Boston itself had a well-developed lesbian feminist community by 1974, and it was one of my greatest pleasures to travel off to the local women's bookstore in Chelsea and buy a myriad of books on lesbian life and liberation.

My partner found a job in a nursing home as a recreational director and provided much of our living expenses while we lived in a spacious and airy two bedroom apartment in Brighton. I will always remember the big ledge we had at the bottom of our picture window overlooking downtown Boston. My partner had a green thumb to be sure and she filled our shelf with plants that thrived with the morning sun. Her job was very humble compared to her educational background but she never complained about this. Jobs were hard to come by in the mid-1970's for all of us Baby Boomers who had poured out of colleges and graduate schools, with Ph.D.'s, with many having to resort to driving cabs to remain in that wonderful Hub City.

During this last year of my theological studies, I connected my partner up with the Board of Ministries from my conference and before 1975 was out, she had been ordained a deacon in the United Methodist Church serving two rural parishes only 70 miles from where I would be serving in the same denomination. On my graduation day from Boston University School of Theology, I walked along the Charles River with my former hometown pastor who had become my mentor in the ministry. I was told I had great potential within the church - that I could become the first woman district superintendent in my conference and perhaps in the years ahead, even a bishop in the UMC. "No other woman I know has your educational background and personality, Martha. You're so well suited for leadership in the church," he said. I was flattered, but wondered even then how all this would be accomplished without giving up my relationship with my partner. Such lofty levels of leadership in the UMC would never be my fate. God had another plan for my life that would slowly and sometimes painfully reveal itself over the next eight years as I moved from the ordained ministry into the legal profession.

Before we left Boston for our respective parishes we privately exchanged marriage vows and we both wore rings the other had given. I had no doubt I was married to my partner and wanted to remain so forever. I wasn't quite certain how this would all play out as we lived 70 miles apart in the years ahead, but I believed it was possible to continue our marriage, and I had every intention of doing so.

We would spend the next two years seeing each other most Sunday nights and taking every available vacation together. In those years before e-mail and cell phones, we often wrote each other every single day. I had a habit of completing a letter late in the afternoon each day and walking to the local post office to place it in the evening mail. There was no question I seemed to have more trouble with our daily separation than did my partner. I often got very depressed being apart from her and told her so. I often wondered during that time in the ministry how long I could continue to live separated from Victoria. She was understanding and wrote to me on Valentine's Day, just a few months into our separation:

February 14, 1976

"My dear Martha,

God knows I love you - there seems to be no way to fully get that across to you - particularly when you are in one of your depressed moods. I wish I could afford to rent one of those planes that writes messages in the sky . . . I love you darling! I'd have it fly over a certain parsonage at 9:30 in the morning and 6 at night every day of the year - until I can be with you at 9:30 and 6 and tell you myself . . . I love you. I love **you**.

You - my lover - the one person I really care about - the one person I want to be with forever - the woman who makes me proud to be me - proud to have her love me when she could love so many others - it makes me cry to thing of it ever ending - so please don't let us let it.

Honey, God brought us together by a set of miraculous circumstances. I really believe that - when I think of that first night - of the fact that I hadn't planned on going to the women's meeting at all - that at the last minute we had a free hour because an unknown group arrived and claimed the stage - the very hour of that meeting - and that I even decided to go then - and the immediate understanding we had between us - God's gift. That I could listen to you beyond all the hurt of that place, the hurt that made me oblivious to so many others ....

The miracle of you staying at Princeton when you got accepted for transfer to Harvard, and our growing love ... the women's center you started and the nights we spent listening to each other, embracing each other's hearts - and then the day we realized our lives would be lived together - our first night together in a tiny dorm bedroom - - - our first Christmas - the ring you gave me - and <u>our</u> little tree - a whole night awake in love in January - do you remember? Your birthday and an emerald green ring I gave you?

Maybe right now we can't be together every day . . . maybe it's hard to last out the lonely days and lonely nights - - - maybe we get depressed and feel like it will never end - - - but sweetheart we will look back on this some day as a time when we learned a lot about how much our love means to us . . . a time when we learned more about ourselves as individuals so that we will be healthier and more in love when we are together. Hard to wait, hard to be patient, but the fact of it being hard will make it <u>more precious</u> when are together, full-time.

So sweetheart, when you get down and blue remember that your honey still loves you and wants to hold you close to her heart. Let me

I love you . . . Happy Valentine's . . . Your lover, Victoria"

During my years in the parish ministry, besides the separation from Victoria, I was also tormented by my hypocrisy of hiding in the closet - pretending to be a single, straight woman. However, some of this pain was diffused by my preoccupation of gaining acceptance just as a woman pastor. As related below, gaining acceptance was not without substantial stress and pain. I told myself that before I could ever consider "coming out" in the church I needed to prove myself as a woman minister first, without the added label of "lesbian woman."

I attended our annual church conference in late May 1975 when I would be formally appointed to my two parishes. I was so conflicted about where my life was headed. On the one hand, I would now get a chance to serve God every day in my own parish, but yet be separated from the person I considered my life partner. I wrote of this anguish in my journal as I attended that conference in May 1975:

> "This was the second day of our Annual Conference session
> and I am in pain over this morning's proceedings. Here I am
> a United Methodist clergy woman at my first conference as
> an ordained pastor, confronting myself with the question of
> why I remain in an institution that condemns homosexuals as

ordained clergy. I am a closeted lesbian - wholly and purely in a monogamous love relationship with another woman. I am so lonely at this moment, as I sit in my room writing all this down. I have temporarily sacrificed my 'marriage' to serve an institution that is slow in Christian charity for those, like me, who know a different truth about the possibility of completely loving a person of one's own sex. Of course, the church is just one of many hostile institutions but it is nevertheless the institution I have chosen to serve.

The bishop this morning compared homosexuals to alcoholics and adulterers! I remain silent to such unenlightened observations - it is difficult to live with myself. But I have thrown myself into the loving hands of the Creator who made me as I am. I do not understand why God guided me into this conflict. Yet, I know equally well that I have been called to ministry and to love this woman to whom I have committed my earthly love. I trust God will sustain me in the months ahead but I still wonder how.

I have submitted my homosexual love to the scrutiny of my Lord and have received no negative response. I pray daily that God will provide me with an answer, a way to live this contradiction between personal revelation that all is good about our love - and the negative response from my church regarding homosexuality. I feel like crying loudly tonight, "Lord, Lord, why hast thou forsaken me?"

CHAPTER TWO

A New Chick In Town

My appointment to my two little parishes by the bishop of my conference took a very circuitous route considering the polity of the United Methodist Church. I would learn from this experience that there were "special rules and qualifications" applied to women candidates to the ministry no matter what the United Methodist Book of Discipline might say.

It was late in April 1975 and I was home from seminary for the weekend when the district superintendent called me on a Saturday afternoon with sudden news of two prospective parishes. I was told over the telephone that there were certain individuals in the two churches who were resistant to the idea of having a woman pastor but that "if you could go down there tomorrow morning and preach to them, I think they might have a change of heart." After the church service I was to meet with the pastor-parish relations committee and unfortunately the district superintendent would not be able to be there with me because he had "other duties to attend to." I agreed to do as he asked, for I was anxious for a church home.

It was many years later when I had time to reflect about how this whole matter was handled that I actually processed, and took in for the first time, the incredible sexism at operation in that time and place. The United Methodist Church was not, and never has been, of a "congregational" format where the ministers are voted upon by the parish after a sermon presentation. The polity of episcopacy, after which the United Methodist Church is patterned, is that ministerial assignments will be made by the bishop, that each parish will be provided a pastor, and that while congregational and ministerial preferences are not ignored outright, those preferences will stand aside for the ultimate decision by the bishop. In a very real sense, the whole theory of United Methodist Church polity was thrown aside in my case, and I was "candidated" for the pastorate of those two small parishes.

In addition, it would become more obvious to me in the years ahead the tremendous stress I was placed under in this "candidating" experience insofar as I had to prove myself in one sermon to a semi-hostile congregation. Several of the church leaders had expressed their belief that they didn't know if they "could stand to hear a woman preach," and the lay leader of the larger parish expressed his conviction that the holy scriptures proscribed women from preaching. On top of having to preach this one sermon, I would face the pastor parish relations committee all alone for the first time - something that just never happened. There is no doubt in my mind that the district superintendent had "other things to attend to" that day because he was afraid to be there with me.

But, I was the proverbial babe in the woods. So with innocence and conviction I set about writing a sermon I would preach in less than 16 hours, that would somehow convince reluctant parishioners that a woman preacher might have something worthwhile to say. My father was sensitive to my predicament, perhaps more than I, and asked if he might drive me to this parish the next morning, some 100 miles from my hometown. I graciously accepted the offer and early Sunday morning we were off to the challenge of a lifetime.

I chose to wear a clerical collar that day because I thought it important for the congregation to face me head on with all the prejudiced negativity they might have on the issue of a woman pastor. It was interesting that as I entered the church that morning and introduced myself to various members of the congregation, that most would not look me in the eye but stared at my clerical collar. These parishes had been without a pastor for a few weeks since their former pastor had been transferred to a needier congregation. The retired pastor who had preached for them in the interim greeted me enthusiastically, and to his credit, this sweet, tender and saintly man did everything he could to make the experience less intimidating for me. He handled the liturgy and gave me a very warm introduction.

I can remember lots of "butterflies" in my life, but none so vivid as the butterflies I felt as I stood before the well-filled sanctuary. Sitting in nearly the front row was the lay leader, pad in hand, ready to take notes on my sermon. As I glanced over the congregation I didn't see many smiling faces except for that of my father, who sat alone, off to the right side of the church. The members had not welcomed him any more than they had welcomed me.

I can recall a few significant occasions in my life when the peace of God filled my soul and gave me strength to go on, but no moment so vivid with God's spirit than the first five minutes of that sermon. I preached on the basic theme that God's kingdom was within our midst - in our hearts - present in our fellowship together. The Old Testament text was about the building of the Tower of Babel, and man's futile attempt to reach God in the heavens. As those first few moments of the sermon revealed themselves I felt empowered with a force far beyond my own life experience. With confidence and emotion

I worked through those fifteen minutes, drawing upon the best form my homiletics training at Princeton, and relying upon God to help me with the rest. Heartstrings were touched as I saw several parishioners, along with my father, wiping tears from their eyes. They had felt God's Spirit there, too.

When the service was done, I adjourned to the back room of the church to meet with the pastor-parish relations committee. There were the anticipated questions about why I had chosen the ministry as a vocation, and what my biography entailed generally. There was an uneasiness in the room until a short, stocky man spoke on behalf of the smaller congregation I would be serving - not the particular church I had preached in that morning. However, many, including this lay leader of the smaller congregation had decided to travel down the hill to the larger parish to hear my sermon.

"Well Rev. Bellinger, I've heard you preach and I must say I haven't heard a better sermon. As I was telling my wife on the way over here this morning to hear your sermon. I don't know what all the fuss is about having a woman minister because personally I don't know where our church would be today if it weren't for all the work our women do in it. I can say on behalf of our church that we'd be proud to have you as our pastor." God sends angels into our lives all the time to help us through difficult times. This man was one of God's angels who would become a dear friend throughout my brief stay in these parishes. With his words, I felt the muscles in my neck and back loosen for the first time and I knew I would get through this.

After his statement to me, others on the parish pastor relations committee began to focus on my family background, my experience in the United Methodist Church before I went to college and seminary, and what I thought my focus in the parish would be. It was easy to tell them about the wonderful job my parents had done in bringing me up in the life of the church, and that if they chose me to be their minister surely a large focus would be to use my own relative youth to reach out to the whole community and develop a large ecumenical youth group. The chairwoman of the pastor-parish relations committee, who had remained relatively silent during our meeting, spoke up and said, "That's exactly what our church needs, more young people, and an ecumenical effort to get all the town's youth involved in constructive activities." She turned to me and smiled warmly. Later in the process I would have this woman as my next door neighbor at the parsonage and we would have many long, enjoyable chats on her veranda in the summer, drinking freshly made lemonade with her special recipe sugar cookies.

I left that village with my father somewhat optimistic. He told me how proud he was of my sermon and asked me how things had gone during the meeting with the pastor-parish committee. "Well, it is in God's hands now," he stated, "but I think you changed some minds today about women in the ministry. The woman sitting not far from me came over after the service, and inquired if you were my daughter. When I told her you most certainly were my daughter she smiled and commented that she had been among the first women to vote in her generation, and it was 'about time' that women be allowed in the pulpit." This woman was 90 years old, kept her own home, still played the piano, and was among the first to invite me to dinner after arriving in the parish - a dinner she cooked all by herself replete with blackberry pie.

Later that night I would receive a call from my "missing in action" district superintendent saying that miraculously there had been a unanimous decision of the committee to accept me as their minister and that I would be assigned the church in June, following annual conference. It was probably more than coincidence that my mentor in the ministry had also retired to a summer home on a lake nearby my parish and would officially be part of my congregation. I'm sure he had something to do with getting me the opportunity to preach and be considered for that appointment putting in a good word with the district superintendent and bishop. When I left the ministry two years later, my mentor would be greatly disappointed with my decision and would send me a very direct and somewhat harsh condemnation of my decision. He would be dumbfounded by my decision to leave, and I would be too closeted to tell him the reason why.

My second day after moving into the parsonage, I decided it was time to see the inside of my second church - the "four corners" parish. There was something very special about journeying to that small church on a week day with no one else around - about opening the door and stepping inside the completely silent sanctuary and walking toward the pulpit I would occupy for the first time on Sunday. I sat for a few moments in a pew, staring at the cross in the center of the altar, asking for God's wisdom to be able to say something meaningful to the people who would sit here come Sunday.

As I exited the church that afternoon, a repairman from the local utility company pulled his truck into the church driveway, rolled down his window and shouted, "Hey, lady, I hear you got a young chick coming in here real soon to preach. 'Spose she'll be any good?" "I don't know," I chuckled back, "Why don't you come Sunday and find out if I am any good."

There were many experiences in my parish ministry which affirmed my sense of fulfillment as a woman pastor but none as powerful as my pastoral relationship with Karl, a middle-aged many dying of leukemia. Karl's diagnosis and rapid decline coincided with my arrival in the parish. His wife had been a faithful member of the parish but Karl had been among the countless husbands steadfastly staying away from church involvement. But when the diagnosis was given, and a new pastor hit town, half out of desperation and half out of curiosity, Karl started coming to my church. Over the next few months I would visit him at home and in the hospital as he sank into physical oblivion.

Two days before he died I went to the hospital to see him. His family left the room so that we could privately talk about his spiritual concerns. As soon as everyone had left the room, Karl grabbed my arm and began to sob, expressing his terror and despair over coming to the end of his life. I was 25 years old with few words of wisdom to offer. But I took Karl in my arms and cradled him as he let all the emotion flow through body wracking sobs. Even though I said nothing, when he stopped crying and put his head back on his pillow he remarked, "Oh, thank you so much, Pastor Marti, you've been such a good friend." I wiped away my own tears as he watched. "I'm going to miss you, Karl," I said. "You don't know what a good friend you've been to me - you've given me reason to go on being who I am - you were one of the first parishioners to really support my ministry. We've been on an adventure you know. You've been moving closer to seeing God, and I have been navigating through the unchartered waters of a woman in ministry. We've been brother and sister through a very frightening time. I really do believe, Karl, that you will see God soon because you are a kind and gentle soul - I will never, never forget you, Karl."

Shortly after that conversation, Karl lapsed into a coma. His wife expressed concern that Karl had never been baptized. I remember telling her that: "God takes his own home, no matter what rite of passage words we say here on earth. Karl's one of God's own. He needs no passwords for eternity."

I've never forgotten Karl. He taught me that real ministry was not about church budgets, or blockbuster sermons. Ministry is about the one-on-one touching of souls, supporting one another through the obstacles of life. True ministry requires no ordination; it only requires that we allow ourselves to be a vessel for God's unconditional love.

It was very difficult for many to even conceive of the idea of a woman in the pulpit in that rural area in 1975. The assumption was made by those who had not heard of my appointment, that the person inhabiting the parsonage reflected God's masculine image. One evening shortly after my arrival to the parish, the parsonage doorbell rang and I answered the door finding an elderly man standing on my front porch. "May I help you?" I inquired. "Why yes, young lady. Can you tell me if your father is home?" With what must have been a slight grin on my face I replied, "Could be that he is, sir, but since that would be about 100 miles from here I couldn't rightly say whether he is home or not." The man stood dumbfounded and I could see, a little bit more than annoyed at my reply.

In an exasperated voice, the old man tried again, "Young woman, would you please tell me whether or not Rev. Bellinger is at home this evening?" I tried to wipe the grin off my face and replied softly, "You're looking at Rev. Bellinger, sir. How may I help you?" I'll never know what was on that gentleman's mind - why he had need of a pastor so late at night. He merely replied, "I don't think you could ever possibly help me," and quickly trotted off into the night. Some 34 years after that experience, I wonder if that old man has met my friend Karl on the other side of life and chatted about the pastoral help he sought but ultimately turned down when the pastor did not present herself in the form he expected.

One of the many duties assigned to me as a parish minister was a monthly church service I was to lead at a large local nursing home. My first service there brought the usual mixture of the curious and critical stares by the worshipers as I led them through the service. It was no doubt especially startling for these octogenarians to have a young woman presenting herself to them as a member of the cloth. Fortunately, my habit of taking my guitar along to lead people in song softened the blow to their sensitivities a bit, and most lustily joined in singing some old hymns, forgetting all about the sex of the person leading them in worship.

After the very first service at the nursing home I was greeting the residents as they filed out the door and a very elderly gentleman, leaning heavily on a cane, approached me with a determined look on his face and stated: "Ma'am, you should know I think you are defying God's laws and scripture by posing as a parson. But while I can't agree with all you said today in your message, I must say I heard every word of it." With that comment he shook my hand and toddled off to his room.

As mortals, when we hear about one of the many labels that inevitably become attached to an individual, such as his or her race, religious persuasion, or sexual orientation, we make certain assumptions about that person whether they are deserved or not. It was no different for me in the assumptions I initially made about the Roman Catholic priest, Father Joe, who lived in the rectory directly across from my parsonage. I mean, after all, here I was a woman in ministry and if there was a church who had made a clearer statement against the ordination of women than the Roman Catholic Church I wasn't aware of it. So I assumed Father Joe would not be readily welcoming me to the ecumenical fold that had been created in the last ten years in the small village in the foothills of the Adirondack Mountains. My assumptions could not have been more incorrect.

Father Joseph was in his last parish before retirement, and given the dearth of priests and the reluctance to retire them much before their 80th birthday, you can imagine Father Joe was well into his golden years. Another assumption I made upon learning of his advanced years was that he would be inflexible and resistant to change. But almost from the beginning, Father Joe welcomed me with a genuinely hearty handshake of friendship. Throughout my time in that parish he would invite me to the rectory for dinner, for coffee cake and conversation, he would participate in an ecumenical wedding held in my church, and even invite me in full clerical garb, to participate in a funeral service in his church. I had made an acquaintance with one of his parishioners who had been very sick in the hospital for several weeks. Her nephew attended my church and told me about his aunt, so every time I went to the hospital to visit my parishioners I would stop in to see her.

When this Roman Catholic aunt passed on, Father Joe said, "You know, Martha, Mildred loved your visits with her at the hospital. She kept telling me every time I visited her that you had been in to say hello, and that she had never had a minister of another faith pay so much attention to her. I think it is only appropriate that you say a few words as we celebrate her life through the funeral mass. Would you come and help me celebrate her funeral mass?" I didn't have to be asked twice, and this was surely one of the more memorable experiences in that parish.

Upon the celebration of the Bicentennial in 1976, I had a party at the parsonage and even hired a band to play some old and new tunes in the gigantic formal living room I had in my parsonage. While I cut the music and party off well in advance of 10 p.m., apparently some of my neighbors phoned Father Joe and complained about the party going on in the Methodist parsonage. "Wasn't it just scandalous that a Methodist minister was acting in this manner?" Through the grapevine I heard about the complaints to Father Joe and his response, "Of course there is nothing wrong with a party in the Methodist parsonage. If I knew she was serving alcoholic beverages, I'd be there myself!"

For the thirteen years following my departure from that parish until his death, Father Joe would send me a Christmas card and write a note each time telling me how proud he was that I had gone to law school in California and was doing so well. He would often inquire of my former parishioners if they had heard from me and how I was doing in law school. When good reports would come back he would say to them, "That's my girl!"

The two parishes I served had memberships of 400 and 80 respectively. The larger parish had recently built a new sanctuary and was substantially in debt for this project. It would be my job to get the money rolling in, and pay off this indebtedness of the larger parish as well as just keeping the doors of the smaller church open. The smaller church was one of the thousands that had been built by Methodist congregations in the early 19th century, a small edifice on the four corners of a hamlet which now consisted of a few homes, a fire station, and a very tiny country store. My most pleasurable moments would be spent in this smaller congregation due to the love and support that surrounded one there by the remaining faithful.

I use the term "remaining faithful" because at my first administrative board meeting in that small church, the lay leader sadly handed me a piece of paper and stated: "Rev. Bellinger, I'm embarrassed to even hand you this. I want you to know it doesn't represent the opinions of those of us here tonight. But you need to see this."

I read the opening sentences of what was the resignation of the secretary of the Administrative Board of the church. Apparently, she along with several other families were leaving this parish because of my appointment as pastor. The letter was replete with all the Pauline passages condemning a woman's vocal participation and leadership in Christ's church.

It would be explained to me that in an adjoining town, an independent Baptist church had sprung up led by a fundamentalist preacher who was telling others I must be a messenger from Satan since women were prohibited from ministry by the Holy Scriptures. It was this pastor's practice to raid other churches of their members to fill his own. He had made a diligent door-to-door campaign to do just that in my little parish as soon as he heard of my appointment. This was several weeks before I even arrived at my parish.

The resignation and accompanying membership loss hurt, but it was not something for which I was totally unprepared theologically. As the first Director of the Princeton Theological Seminary's Women's Center, and an ardent Christian feminist, I had been made aware of these fundamentalist beliefs, and knew the appropriate theological counter arguments. But it was hard to argue to those who had already left the church before even hearing one of my sermons or meeting me face-to-face. I knew they were wrong, but I felt the sting of rejection nevertheless. At age 25, your desire to please others can be overwhelming and criticism is very hard to take even when completely unjustified.

But God would demonstrate the ultimate power of a committed faith community through that tiny band of supportive congregants who remained behind for "Pastor Marti." For every member who had left because of my appointment, two new members joined. The number of youth attending the church greatly increased. We were in a much better position spiritually and financially when I left that parish than before my appointment. We see God's provision and grace most keenly after a healthy dose of adversity. This is the history of the true followers of Christ, one of struggle and eventual triumph in the midst of opposition - most especially opposition from those very people who call themselves God's children. Faith is purified and sanctified through confrontation with inhumanity and exclusivity.

As for the larger congregation we had no real money problems. Money rolled in to pay off the debt on the new church structure. We kept our denominational dues current, and had some money left over to meet our conference mission obligations.

In my small corner of the world I suddenly realized there was a social mission I had to help the community address. After more people than I wanted to think about kept showing up at my parsonage asking for money for food to feed their families, I did a little investigation to try and determine if there was indeed a poverty problem in what appeared to be a pristine, prim and proper environment. I soon learned two significant facts. One fact was that during the winter months when tourism and logging shut down, as many as a third of the work force was thrown out of work in surrounding communities. The other fact was that in my own parishes, the main employer who manufactured shoes, would often lay people off without pay for a least a two week period in the summer and winter, with the winter lay off coming right over the Christmas holidays. For people already living on minimum wage in an environment where heating fuel was astronomical in the winter, and groceries were no cheaper than anywhere else in New York State, this was a disaster. People did indeed run out of money for food, or sometimes had to make a choice between keeping warm and not freezing to death, or not eating and remaining hungry. This was particularly true for the elderly as well on fixed incomes who could not afford to be cold and felt they could risk malnutrition instead.

I first took the problem to our ecumenical group of pastors and told them that I thought we needed to organize some effort to address this problem. They were in agreement. In fact, one of our fellow clergymen had such a small salary to support his wife and three children that they often had meatless meals several times a week. "What could we do they asked?" I suggested we start a modest food bank. Our ecumenical group could prepare a list of foodstuffs essential to a good diet. We would suggest to our parishioners they select an item or items from the list which they could donate, or in the alternative, they could donate money to help replenish our pantry with these needed foods. We could centralize the distribution from the large pantry in my parsonage. People with food needs would be directed to my home, and when I was not there, we could have a local grocer give them $15 worth of basics to get them by. We would call it the Ecumenical Food Pantry.

It seemed like such a simple, humane project, I was not prepared for the opposition I would encounter, some of it from my own parishioners. Several congregants couldn't understand why we needed this. What was welfare all about anyway and didn't we subsidize the impoverished enough through our tax dollars? There were too many already receiving free rides in our country. Why encourage more to jump on board the welfare wagon? The local factories paid a decent wage, they said. If these people would just stop spending their money on booze and color TV sets, they wouldn't go hungry. I was appalled at some of the callousness and replied that I had already been in homes where senior citizens were either freezing or starving. I told them that the children of alcoholics were just as entitled to food as their children were and that these children could not control their parents' finances to make sure there was peanut butter and white bread to eat. Hadn't Christ admonished his disciples to "suffer the little children" to come unto him first and foremost? Weren't children what the Kingdom of God was all about? How could we let them starve for the sins of their parents? Maybe scripture did say that the sins of the fathers would be visited upon their sons, but this did not mean we were to stand by with detachment and let hunger and poverty destroy a young life when we could do something about it. The final argument hit home. It was hard to drink up white bread and peanut butter. We were not going to be distributing money to these needy folks, but rather food, and if some old drunk thought about pawning that food, the resale market for day old bread, peanut butter and powdered milk was not high.

The groceries and money started to come in consistently and

generously - especially from our Roman Catholic parish. Say what you might about the Vatican and its gold and ermine but on the local level, most Catholics knew what it meant to reach out to the poor and needy. Now when people came to my door on a cold winter's night desperate to feed their kids, they were given at least two or three bags of food. We also started a large Thanksgiving and Christmas basket program so that families had something a little extra to eat on those days while the rest of us enjoyed sumptuous meals at our respective families' tables.

Years after I left those parishes I would get newspaper clippings from some of my former parishioners attesting to the continuing success of the Ecumenical Food Pantry. If I did nothing else of value with my time in those two small towns, the food pantry was it. To this day it is hard for me to think of people hungry, particularly children. Perhaps God will use me again one day to help feed the poor. In the meantime I encourage everyone to give generously to any legitimate program which feeds the poor. Christ saw the importance of feeding the multitudes both spiritually and physically.

One of the area morticians had attended my parish before I was assigned to the church. Once I arrived he stopped attending my church, expressing outright to my district superintendent that he believed a woman could not properly officiate at funeral services - that it would just not look right to have a woman giving these final rites. The man had a son at West Point and another about to go to West Point, and was about as "macho" as one could get. At least he was honest to my face in conveying these same thoughts while nevertheless moving forward with funerals my families expected me to perform. We worked professionally together quite well. He learned that most of time I knew what I was doing and could perform a meaningful funeral service when required.

I wish I could relate that when it was time for me to leave the parish that this man had made a turn around in his attitudes about women in the ministry. But I don't believe he did. I will say that when I left that parish he respected me as an individual, and that meant a lot. He came to realize that even though he honestly told me I had no business being in that parish, that I expressed no animosity toward him and in fact continued to refer some parishioners to him for his services. He came to understand early on that his words of discouragement would not dissuade me from my ministry.

Love and acceptance is a wonderful thing, and it is what we all strive for so mightily in our journey. But I have come to realize in the later years of my life what is absolutely essential for every human being is that they attain respect from their colleagues, peers, friends, and most especially from loved ones. Of course, we cannot get respect from others until we respect ourselves and now that I am older, I understand that this is what our mission in life is all about. It has taken to this last third of my life to understand how important respect is, and that I would prefer it every time to supposedly being loved and accepted. For only God guarantees us unconditional love, and unless one allows him or herself to be filled with this kind of love, the best one human being can give another is respect.

Even though Victoria had declared her undying love for me many times, she struggled with what it would be to be labeled as lesbian, and whether this was her true nature. Having the perspective of hindsight I now realize that she was truly bisexual. When I first met her at Princeton, months before we became intimately involved, she was truly infatuated with one of our male seminarians who did not return the interest. He was very nice to her but clearly not interested in having a boyfriend-girlfriend relationship with her. For many weeks I listened to her longing to be with him as a girlfriend, and commiserated with her pondering as to why he didn't find her attractive. Silently I could only think at the time, I can't imagine what's wrong with him - those beautiful green eyes of yours and your delightful laugh - who could resist you?

As our friendship deepened and my interest in her was very clear, her desire to be with this man lessened to the point where she no longer talked about him, and the thought that she might well be a lesbian was a concept she seriously entertained and acted upon months later. Nevertheless, the issue of her bisexuality lingered throughout our relationship, but I was too much "in love" with her to acknowledge it or certainly discuss it at all. While in the parish ministry about a year and a half into our separation, the issue arose again in a very intense and threatening manner. Victoria had attended a special seminar for ministers in her conference one week and met a single male minister who expressed a real interest in her. When she returned from this seminar, she called me on the telephone and said she had something to tell me, and she wasn't sure how I would take it. Before she told me the story, my heart was in my throat after my soul intuitively guessed what she was about to tell me.

At this seminar she had spent much time with her male colleague culminating in an intimate encounter which she described as very satisfying and it got her to thinking that maybe she really wasn't a lesbian after all. She went on to relate that she had informed him of our relationship, and that he told her after they had sexual intercourse that there was no way she could be a lesbian and have enjoyed sex with him as much as she did. The term "furious" does not begin to describe my emotion at that time. In my head I thought, "How dare this man who has been with my partner for one week and who has been intimate with her on two occasions tell her she is not a lesbian." What had these past three years of intimacy between us been all about? Was our relationship meaningless, and just a dalliance while she waited for some man to swoop into her life?

My head was spinning and my end of the telephone line became silent. "Martha, are you still there? What are you thinking about all this?" Victoria implored. "I am not sure you want to hear what I have to say, Victoria," I replied in a very sarcastic tone. "I thought our relationship was a committed one and that we were not about experimenting with anyone else, man or woman! Don't you remember the vows we recited to one another? I thought you were better than this. I need to hang up now. There is nothing more for me to say right now." And with those last words, I hung up the receiver and burst into tears.

As badly as I wanted to talk to her some more about this experience she had just had with her colleague, I felt betrayed, deeply hurt and knew I was in no shape to handle a civilized conversation. I tried to bury myself in parish activities - hospital visitations, home visits, ecumenical meetings, sermon preparation. It had always been my practice to bury myself in work whenever something was bothering me emotionally to the point of obsession. Two weeks later, Victoria called my parsonage again.

"Martha, look I know you are probably through with me, and I understand. There is a new wrinkle in this mess." I keyed onto the word "mess." Was she trying to admit she had made a terrible mistake in her unfaithfulness?

"So why is this now a mess for you," I retorted.

"I can hear that anger in your voice, Martha, which is so unlike you but I understand. Just hear me out and if you want to hang up the phone after you listen to me, then I will know where we go from here," Victoria tried to reason.

"I at least owe you the opportunity to explain I suppose," I replied. "So go ahead. What is the mess you are referring to?"

"Well, this guy called me the day after I last talked to you. He said he had not been completely honest with me about his situation. He is engaged to get married in the fall, and while he doesn't discount the special time we had together, he felt it best not to get involved with someone who was equivocal about her sexuality," she reported.

"So that's his story. But where does that leave me?" I inquired. "Do you think you can just pick up where we left off and everything is ok? You hurt me very badly. Despite that hurt I still love you but why should I ever risk more involvement with you?" I wanted her to beg for forgiveness and I would no doubt take her back.

"If you were calculating and reasonable about this, you would not risk any more involvement with me. But, I know you well, Martha, and I know you have a very forgiving heart, especially for idiots. And I was an idiot. I see it all now very clearly. The big mess is that my period is late and I am thinking I may be pregnant. I have an appointment with Planned Parenthood tomorrow for a pregnancy test. I am trying to figure this all out. You know I believe in a woman's right to chose but here I am 27 years old and should have known better. I am not sure I could have an abortion but I don't know where I'd go or what I would do if I am pregnant." The next sound on the telephone line was Victoria's body wracking sobs.

"Look, Victoria. I have no church meetings this evening and can spring away from here for a night. You stay right at your parsonage and I'll be there in about two hours so we can discuss this face to face." I hung up the phone, left a message on my parsonage door about how I could be reached, and phoned the lay leader explaining I needed to tend to a sick ministerial friend out of town and would be back the next day.

As I drove to Victoria's parsonage the thoughts came to mind a mile a minute. God, this was a mess. How could she have been so foolish? Victoria was better than this stunt! Had she risked all this so that she would be forced to choose heterosexuality! Was she so naive as to equate sexual intercourse with commitment from a man? Having been a co-ed at a large university I knew better. Maybe because she had spent her college years at a women's college, she didn't. A baby! There was no place for a baby in her occupation and circumstance. Either her profession had to go, or the baby had to go. Where did this put me? How ostracized I would be just by being her friend and helping her have this baby if she chose. She wouldn't be able to stay with me in the ministry, and I would have to chose her or my own calling.

By the time I pulled in her driveway I was thoroughly worked up. But when I saw her standing on her porch, holding the door open for me, a forlorn look on her face, my anger and fear faded quickly, and as usual, Martha was off to the rescue. Once inside the parsonage I enfolded her in my arms as she sobbed on my shoulder. "It's okay," I kept repeating. "We'll figure it out together." We had a cup of tea together, Victoria's favorite beverage of choice. I inquired what time her appointment with Planned Parenthood would be the next day and if she wanted me to go with her. She said she'd be fine to go on her own and thought she should bear that responsibility herself. She said they would know within a few days if the pregnancy test was positive.

That night I held her closely but there was no lovemaking. It seemed out of place and unnatural to me then. I was uncomfortable that someone else had held her and been intimate with her when I believed she had committed herself to me forever. Oh yes, how strong and yet unrealistic first love can be. I still wasn't sure about my own feelings except that I did still love her very much and she was right, I would forgive this huge indiscretion as a faithful friend would. I told her that I would stand by whatever decision she made should she discover she was pregnant. I would even go off with her someplace, try to find a job, and support us all. She had decided she would never let the father know of his child given his very insensitive last contact with her. I agreed he didn't deserve to ever know.

I left the next morning and headed back to my parish, knowing that our future, whatever that might be, hung in the balance. Later that morning when I opened my purse in my parsonage I found a small white envelope addressed "Martha Emily." Victoria had extraordinary handwriting and it was always a treat to receive any written communication from her. To this day, I occasionally pull out her old correspondence just to marvel at its beauty. The small envelope contained a note which read: "Thank you for being you. I love you with everything I have inside to give. No matter the results of my examination, I am yours. Trust me . . . . God will help us work all the 'things out' . . . a love as deep as this, that can last through all of this, must be Gods . . . . Call me when you can. I love you . . . ." Sometime early in the morning before I had awoken at her home she must have written this and stuck it in my purse.

A few days later we would learn the pregnancy test was negative and our collective sighs of relief were followed by thank you to God's plan which had not included this puzzle for us to figure out so early in our relationship and our ministerial careers. Would I have left the ministry with her had she been pregnant and tried to pull us together as a family somewhere? There is no doubt in my mind I would have done that. I had turned down a transfer and full scholarship to Harvard to remain with her while she finished her last year of seminary. I had given up a very prestigious Princeton preaching scholarship which would have required me to remain at Princeton after she graduated and yet, I had transferred to Boston University instead so we could start a new life together. Why wouldn't I have sacrificed some more? I loved her beyond all else. She was my destiny. But God had other plans for us, for me, and so the sacrifice never had to be made.

CHAPTER THREE

A Bend In The Road

For several months after the pregnancy scare, my life settled into the normalcy I had grown to hate. Waking up in the morning in an empty bed, only to trudge down to a cold and drafty parsonage kitchen and living room to sip some coffee and try to remember what was on the agenda for today's ministerial tasks. I lived for our Sunday nights and Monday mornings together. I kept myself very busy out of necessity. There was just me in this parish. My predecessor had been a married man whose wife fulfilled many parish tasks. As a woman minister the expectations were that I would do it all. I would visit the sick, the homebound, counsel the confused, preach two sermons a Sunday, lead the ecumenical youth group, attend the ecumenical church meetings, show up at the many church committee meetings each month, oversee the food pantry's operation and be available for all the funerals, weddings and other life events a parson was supposed to attend.

I thought I was keeping up well with my duties until a woman parishioner started to become very critical of my lack of attendance at all the church women's group meetings. These meetings had always been on Monday evenings, the one full day of rest I tried to take off each week, and of course, my precious time with Victoria. When I heard the complaints about my absence from these meetings, I was reminded that my predecessor's wife never missed a meeting so why shouldn't I be there? My response was to cut my Mondays short with Victoria and make sure I was back in town by 7 p.m. to attend the monthly women's meeting. When you are in your twenties, no matter your occupation, you want to please, and please you try to do at every turn.

But while I did like the close interaction I had with my parishioners, especially in times of death or sickness, and I thoroughly enjoyed putting together a good sermon for which I became well known, I was lonely, and confused, and angry. My denominational periodicals began to arrive with more and more articles about how the United Methodist Church should address the gay rights movement. Most certainly it was clear to all the columnists that the Boards of Ordination should begin to inquire of new ordinands as to their "sexual preference," and remain strong in our Book of Doctrine's statement that: "Homosexuality is inconsistent with Christian faith." The incoming news was menacing in nature with a witch-hunt flavor for anyone who was conspicuously single. The albatross of hypocrisy hung heavier and heavier on my neck.

I didn't fear discovery. Many in my parishes knew about my fine Upstate United Methodist parents and connections. I was the wholesome farm girl, who knew how to dress appropriately and wear a bit of eye makeup. No one would ever suspect I was a lesbian. I had even become good friends with the single male Unitarian minister in town, who had originally come from California and was divorced. We would often have mid-morning coffee together in the main café of the village, and even went to the Shriner's Ball together. Everyone complimented me on my beautiful dress and what great dancers Marvin and I appeared to be. But I never told Marvin about my relationship with Victoria and he was interested in nothing more than friendship. It was very obvious he was still madly in love with his ex-wife and when he first showed me her picture, I could see why. She was stunning, but unwilling to live the life of minister's wife. So he had fled across the country thinking he could forget about her better from a distance.

Marvin was content to let me listen for hours to his ravings about his terrible loss of love while trying to remain true to what he believed was his calling to be a minister. How I wanted to let him know I had a similar struggle and listening to his hurt somehow lessened mine. At least I still had my love in my life once a week, and on vacations. But how long could this go on, I asked myself almost daily.

As the end of my second year in the parish drew to a close, I knew I had to leave the pastorate. I missed being near my partner, and I had extreme difficulty dragging myself into the pulpit appearing to be someone I wasn't. Even though I never even preached a sermon on the church and homosexuality, or even conducted an adult discussion group about the topic, I knew the people in my pews would all walk out the door if they knew my true orientation. To me, God was about honesty, and if you could not even be honest with others about who you really were, what kind of life would you have? The soul starts to die when you live in a closet.

I first had a discussion with my district superintendent and informed him I did not feel the parish ministry was for me but that perhaps I could serve the church in some other capacity such as a chaplain. My district superintendent, as earlier mentioned, was not very liberated in his feelings about women in the ministry and was not about to encourage me to stay. He said he was aware they were looking for a chaplain at my old alma mater, Syracuse University, and my heart lifted. Were I to gain this spot, I would be within fifteen miles of my partner's parish and we could most likely sink into the anonymity of this large residential university with little concern about the nature of our relationship.

I wasted no time in applying for the slot to the very man who had encouraged me to enter the ministry some six years before. He was most pleasant and confirmed that they were indeed looking for their first woman chaplain. But I would learn later that he already had in mind who he wanted in this position, a woman Episcopal priest, one of the first to be ordained in that denomination and a Yale woman to boot. My bishop was not happy with this head chaplain's eventual choice and told me that he had wanted me to fill the spot, but it was not his place to order my appointment since the University had its own independent selection process.

So there was nowhere to go. Having given my district superintendent my clear intention of leaving my parish, I applied to a summer post graduate theological studies program at Harvard Divinity, wondering if I should think about a doctorate in theology. I was accepted into the program without much trouble and then I told my congregations I would be leaving for Cambridge and more studies. It was done. In June I would preach my last sermon and then head off to Cambridge.

What was Victoria thinking? She was emphatic that she was not yet ready to leave her ministry and proceeded on to full ordination that same month within the denomination to which I had brought her for the first time three years before. I sat in the back of the chapel and watched her become ordained as an elder in the ministry, asking myself why she meant so much to me but why I apparently meant so little to her. Of course my mind would not let me fully take in this seeming betrayal. Maybe God had a plan for her in the ministry that God did not have for me? How could I fight that or question that possible design for her life?

The summer after I left the parish was a dark time in my life. Although I had voluntarily left the parish ministry, I felt abandoned by my church and my God. I had no doubt that it was meant for me to be a lesbian, and yet, I could not understand how God had called me to ministry given the lack of acceptance of my sexual orientation by the church. If God wanted me to be a prophet about this issue, why hadn't God equipped me with the courage to "come out?" I was already exhausted from having to prove myself as a woman minister, how could I ever take on this new identification that would surely end my career in theology?

I felt like a complete failure in life. I made myself so sick I ended up in the Harvard Medical Center for several days vomiting and becoming totally dehydrated. I never told anyone in my family about this hospitalization. What would I say was the cause? I laid in bed in that medical center for five days asking God to take me. I had no answers as to where my life was headed and what it was all about. I did have one dear college friend who lived in Boston and came to see me a couple times at the medical center. I was "out" to her and she understood my inner torment. She had no problem with my being gay and tried to help me think about new directions for my life. She may well have been the thread that kept my sanity and health intact. How often I have found this to be in my life when feeling alone and drifting with little purpose. Out of the blue the phone rings, a letter arrives, a personal visit is made from a friend who is checking on my welfare. This has brought me back from the brink of oblivion on more than one occasion. From these experiences I have learned to never fail to do this for your friends when you know they are hurting. Do not stay away, nor be overly intrusive, just listen and accept them for who they are, and let them know you love them.

When I got out of the Medical Center I was able to get caught up in my summer studies program and even earned an "A." I had proved to myself I could succeed at Harvard but that is not what I really wanted. For now, I was tired of theological studies, and lost as to the purpose of it all. While at Harvard that summer, Victoria called a couple times and tried to apologize for her behavior in leaving me on my own. The first time she phoned she said her mother and sister told her she had been very cruel to me and that if they were I, they would feel very hurt and abandoned. We had been out to her family for a couple years and while her mother had some trouble at first adjusting to the idea of our relationship, within time she became a dear friend who always referred to herself as my "Mom."

Victoria's second call was even harder to take and after it was concluded I asked her to call me no more. In this second conversation she talked about having coffee with one of her woman parishioners who was dying of cancer, yet spoke so fondly of how she had been blessed with a wonderful husband and children. Victoria said that afternoon had a profound effect upon her and she began thinking that a traditional family for her was perhaps more realistic. "What do you expect me to say, Victoria? Why are you calling me and telling me all this when you know how much I still love you. Your Mom and sister are right, you can be cruel and don't call me anymore."

When my time at Harvard ended, I decided to return to my parents' home for a brief period so I could help take care of my dear uncle who had just fallen inside his home and broken his neck. Uncle Earl had been like a second father to me. I had been born within six hours of his own birthday and we always had celebrated our birthdays together. He and my aunt had no children of their own, so my sisters and I became their "adopted" children. When this accident occurred he was 69, and at the hospital he required 24 hour nursing care because he was terrified of being alone at night. My aunt, knowing I probably could use some extra money, offered to pay me to stay with him at night which I graciously accepted.

Before I left Cambridge, I had phoned Victoria and told her of my plans and my need to pick up some personal belongings I had stored at her parsonage. She seemed delighted to hear my voice and suggested we might have dinner together after my long drive from Cambridge. When I arrived at her parsonage she was not there but had left a note on the door to go on in the parsonage. That was in a time and location of the 20th century when one had no fear of leaving a door open to one's rural domicile. As I walked in the door, I noticed she had set the dining room table, replete with fine linen, candles, and china.

I sat patiently in the living room for her arrival realizing how helpless and lost I had become. Soon her car pulled in the driveway and I peeked out the curtain to see her carrying a grocery bag. Those three hours I spent with her that evening remain imprinted on my mind as if they had occurred just yesterday and not almost 33 years in the past.

"Well, hi there," she said in a very perky voice. "As usual I am running behind and you are always on time. I wanted to surprise you with a good home cooked meal before you headed home."

"That really wasn't necessary. I thought we'd be dining out," I replied.

"Now I know how much you love my cooking, Martha. And I think I owe you at least that much," Victoria laughed.

She was right. I loved her cooking. Victoria was from genuine Southern gentry which traced its ancestry back to Patrick Henry. The art of fine Southern cooking had also been handed down from daughter to daughter and she could make anything from scratch, especially rolls and biscuits. My mind drifted back to the first meal she ever cooked for me in a tiny little dormitory kitchenette at Princeton before we became lovers.

"Here, have a seat in the kitchen and talk to me while I finish this meal." she directed. "So how is Uncle Earl now? Any change? He is such a sweet man and has loved you so much. What a shame this had to happen to him," she commented as she placed her homemade raised rolls in the oven to cook. I had already smelled the pot roast when I entered her parsonage, a most inviting smell on a rather cool September night.

"They have him in some type of frame which allows them to turn him completely over onto his stomach every few hours. He literally hangs in the air while in this position. It sounds just dreadful and he's frightened to be left alone. So if I can be of help staying with him at night until he is healed, I guess that's the best thing I could do with my life right now."

"Any thoughts about what you might do in the long haul once he is healed?" Victoria inquired as she removed the rolls from the oven.

"I have no idea. Any suggestions for employment for a woman with a bachelor's degree in political science and a master of theology degree," I replied sarcastically.

"Well, enough sadness. Let's just enjoy this meal and time together and put our worries aside for a few hours," Victoria suggested. Easy for her to say, I thought. She's still a minister in her parish with a salary and a purpose for her life.

As I sat across the table from her, she put down her folk and looked me straight in the eye commenting, "I never could resist you when you are wearing that stunning lavender suit you have on." Her bright green eyes twinkled.

I was momentarily without words. What was all this ingratiating behavior by her? Had her "male plans" bombed? It was in her nature to fear complete solitude and if no man was "waiting in the wings" she was no doubt having second thoughts. I recovered my senses enough to reply. "Well if that's the case, I should have purchased this suit earlier and worn it every time I saw you in the past."

"Oh Martha, I don't think that would have helped. You must know I have been so confused about who I am - what I need from life. It really has little to do with how much I respect and love you. We just live in such a non-accepting world - it complicates everything."

"Yes, being gay certainly has its disadvantages, but I don't know how else to be," I replied. "When you find a way to turn off the 'gay part' of yourself, please share. There's not a man I have met or dated who has come close to making me feel the passion I have felt with you, and only you." I emphasized the "only you" part to make her realize once again I had not been the unfaithful one.

We finished our meal with other banter I don't exactly recall so many years later. I do recall she mentioned some of her congregants were beginning to give her problems about wanting to change their form of worship they had for a hundred years and about some of her ideas for social mission in the community. I knew she was in a difficult parish. My Dad had some business experiences with the lay leader of her church, and had told me when he knew Victoria was assigned to that parish that I should be very supportive of her because the lay leader was one of the most difficult men he had every had to deal with in his life. My Dad was very easy going and very hesitant to say bad things about anyone so I knew this lay leader must be a prize! Of course, I was not "out" to my parents then and Dad never knew how much permission this was giving me to spend more of my spare time with Victoria than my own family those two years we were apart.

I do distinctly recall that Victoria asked me if I wanted to spend the evening at her home instead of driving ninety more minutes that evening. Oh how inviting she was. I wanted to take her hand and fly upstairs to the bedroom and forget all that had transpired between us.

But some inner strength allowed me to decline the invitation, making some comment about how staying at her home would only further complicate things for me and so I graciously exited the door with my belongings I had collected earlier.

The time with my uncle was a nightmare. He was suffering so much and as I sat with him through those long nights sometimes with him audibly wincing from pain and begging for sips of water, I wondered what was good about life. To compound the problem, my uncle seemed to be the victim of a very inattentive neurosurgeon, and the family was often arguing over what should be our next course of action in trying to get him well. After about six weeks in the hospital the neurosurgeon believed Uncle Earl was improved enough to be in a halo type neck brace so he could spend his days sitting up in bed normally. My aunt believed my nightly bedside vigils could end as he felt more at ease with the new arrangements.

I phoned Victoria with the news and she sounded very glad to hear from me. I suggested to my parents that I might visit her for a couple days to rest and recover from the many nights I had gone without sleep at my uncle's bedside. They understood this to be a most logical plan and promised to fill me in with any new developments regarding Uncle Earl.

As I drove to Victoria's parsonage, I knew I would try to resume our intimacy with little thought of where that would take me or hurt me more. After watching all that pain and suffering in the hospital, I didn't want to think about anything but warmth and love. And it came to pass that for three days, Victoria and I couldn't get enough of one another. We went out for one romantic meal at a Italian restaurant nearby, and she had to tend to a few parish obligations during those days, but aside from those excursions outside the home, we had shut out the rest of the world and focused on how much we loved one another.

As I write this part of the memoire some 33 years later, Etta James is singing on my i-Pod, "Don't go to strangers, baby, come on home to me." Etta's lyrics specifically encourage her lover to go out "and make his mark for your friends to see, but when you need more than company, don't go to strangers, baby, come on home to me." That pretty much sums up where my mind was drifting those three days with Victoria. Maybe continuing in the ministry for her was a way to make her mark in the world. Personally I couldn't see that for myself given the way the United Methodist Church was drifting in a more conservative tone, but Victoria was different. And, being blindly in love with her, I guess I was willing to drift about until she understood she needed to be with me.

It was just three days after leaving my uncle's side that my father called Victoria's parsonage and asked to speak to me. "Martha, it is my sad duty to tell you Uncle Earl died early this morning." Dad went on to explain that the doctor said Uncle Earl had actually died of a heart attack in his sleep. The several weeks of being hospitalized in various contraptions to try and heal his broken neck had thoroughly warrn out his frail 69 year old heart the doctor had said. I told Dad I'd be home in a few hours.

Victoria was sad for me and asked if I wanted her to drive me home. I declined the offer knowing I needed to be alone. I told her I'd let her know about the funeral arrangements in the event she could get free from parish obligations to attend. She made the calling hours and the funeral and was very considerate and helpful to my family. During that time at home I formulated a plan with a relative to go to Florida and renovate a modest home we would buy with some of their monies, and my withdrawn pension monies from the church.

It had been my uncle's dream to escape the harsh Upstate New York winters and spend time in Florida during those months, and now, as my aunt and parents were aging, we dreamt of a Southern retreat for the whole family.

In my heart, I also knew I had to let Victoria find herself. That well might mean she would choose a male life partner, or choose to remain in the ministry forever. I was arrogant to believe at that time that my love for her would win out in the long haul as it had in the past. I was so young and inexperienced in these matters of the heart. It would take me years to understand all the complications of love with Victoria. So I said goodbye to Victoria on a cold October day in 1977 and headed to Florida by myself.

It was a most unhappy time in Florida. The house we had purchased was more rundown than I had ever imagined and overseeing the renovation was a nightmare. At night I would go to bed to the sound of mice scurrying about the house. I had repainted and thoroughly cleaned one room for my bedroom. As I got deeper into winter, the small space heater for the home barely warmed my Spartan living room, so I scraped together enough money to buy an electric blanket so I could stay warm. I cried myself to sleep more nights than not because I was so lonely with little hope things would get better. The Florida job market was even worse than the national job market which in 1977 was a disaster. What jobs could I possibly fill with a bachelor of arts degree and a master of theology degree. Not many.

I even ventured into the world of employment agencies which would try and find you some marginal job and then take a significant percentage of your first year's earnings for the favor. One "employment counselor," who was blond and beautiful, excoriated me for my conservative dress. "Just look at yourself, Martha, you look like a pastor! Don't you realize you are going to scare off most potential employers when they learn about your religious background! I think we need to soft pedal this religious thing if you are going to have any chance at all at getting a job," she stated in a curt and condescending voice. It was hard for me to believe I was in the land of Anita Bryant where a conservative dress and a cross around your neck could be offensive!

Finally turning to the want ads in the local newspaper I located a job at a tropical fish wholesale company, packaging fish to be shipped to pet stores around the country. It was a minimum wage job for 40 hours and $130 a week. It was exhausting work since I was on my feet eight hours a day with only a half hour for lunch, for which we were not remunerated. My supervisor was a hard edged woman who had never graduated from high school and liked to find fault with even my finest performance in packaging the fish. It was not the hard work that bothered me - as an old farm girl I knew what hard work was all about. Nor did it bother me that my supervisor had not graduated from high school. I kept my own college education a secret. It was just the thought that after seven long years of hard educational endeavor, this was where my life had fallen. I was bitter, lonely, inconsolable.

Just after Christmas 1977, Victoria said she wanted to fly down and see me. Yes, she had missed me, too, and was beginning to encounter some hostile and senseless opposition to her ministry from some of her parishioners and most especially from her district superintendent who had the backbone of a jellyfish. With her visit to Florida came hope. I made a decision to go North again and see if I could put my life together and resume a relationship with her. She was elated with my decision. In late February of 1978 I returned North and looked for work near Victoria's parish while staying with her at her parsonage. It was the time of the Carter administration and the CETA program, a comprehensive education and job training project for those who needed to get into a very problematic job market.

After visiting the New York State Employment Division I found out there was a CETA position for a probation officer in a nearby county. I applied, and through a series of providential events I would learn a month later I was hired. Victoria was overjoyed. She had been hanging on to her position at the parish for financial reasons only. I assured her my new job would pay enough to provide an apartment and food on the table. That's all we required.

And so we moved for a few months into the first floor of a lovely Victorian home in a small town of 5,000 people. Victoria told her parish and district superintendent she was through and moved out of the parish into our apartment. Soon she was able to find a job working for social services in the same county and building where I worked. We set about the business of being nine to five employees and we were living together again every day for the first time in almost three years. For once it seemed like God was making everything work out for us again. While I missed somewhat my ministerial role, I genuinely enjoyed my new vocation as a probation officer. I took a postgraduate course in psychology at Syracuse University.

As the year progressed in my new work, a new thought began to creep into my mind. Why not be a lawyer? Many of the attorneys I saw acting on behalf of the criminal defendants I was supervising seemed inadequate and uncommitted to their client's interests. I thought I could do better, and perhaps as an attorney I could change the world more than I ever imagined as a pastor. It was an option I'd explored as an undergraduate at Syracuse. Maybe it was time to get back to that plan. I had achieved only a mediocre score on my Law School Admission Test (LSAT) as a junior at Syracuse University but maybe now I'd do a little better and set about studying for a new go round on the LSAT.

As I discussed my plan with Victoria she seemed interested in exploring the same option. She admitted that her early vocational testing as a high school student had revealed she was best suited to be an attorney and her father was indeed an attorney. I didn't push her and told her it was her decision to make but that I was going to give the LSAT and my law school application another chance.

Much to my amazement I did much better on the LSAT this time than I had done six years before. No doubt Princeton and Boston University studies had helped a bit. The next decision had to be where to apply to law school. I knew I would have to work during the day and go to law school at night because I could not afford a day program. The availability of nighttime law schools was somewhat limited on the East Coast but much more available on the West Coast. I wanted to go to an American Bar Association accredited school so that when I graduated I could return to New York if I wanted to and take the bar there. I didn't know if I was ready to kiss off the East Coast forever.

The Unitarian minister I had befriended while I was in my parish had a good friend who was a professor of law at a new ABA school in California, Whittier College School of Law which had a night school and also admitted classes in January. Whittier College was well known to the world through Richard Nixon's undergraduate studies there but the school had just recently opened its law school and was looking for good students. I wrote for information, liked what I read and applied. At the same time Victoria was taking her LSAT, sailed through with high scores, and she also applied to Whittier. We were both accepted for January 1979 admission. Now we just needed to wrap up our affairs on the East Coast and go West to start a new chapter in our lives. Victoria was very excited. She had often mentioned to me she thought California would be an exciting place to live and was even more eager to move there than I.

Just before Christmas 1978, we concluded our jobs with the county, said goodbye to my family, loaded up a used Chevy Impala we had purchased for the long trip West, and stopped by Victoria's family home for Christmas before the long trek. We had no place in which to live in California, no jobs, just enough money for the trip and our first semester's tuition. Beyond that, we were traveling on faith.

CHAPTER FOUR

Saying Hello To Socrates

The trip West proved to be a bit arduous. We had planned to take the southern route which we believed would lead us across Route 40 into California. However, we ran into one of the worst ice storms in a decade and had to dip down into Texas and cross over Interstate 10 into the Los Angeles area. I'll never forget the long stretches of barren road in west Texas and wondering if we would ever get out of that state. I'll also always remember the sensation of hitting rush hour traffic almost 60 miles outside of Los Angeles on the widest highways I had ever seen with all the cars traveling about 70 miles an hour in all of the four lanes or more. I had driven all over the United States and in Canada, but nothing prepared me for this. Victoria, having always been an extremely nervous rider, could barely look out the window at the freeway. I assured her it would be okay, and that we'd be at the Motel Six outside L.A. where I had made reservations for a week in just a few minutes.

We checked into our room and collapsed. We'd made it the 2,500 miles but not without a price on our bodies. I pondered in amazement that night about how our ancestors, particularly the women in long skirts on bumpy buckboards and wagons had ever made it to the Golden State. Who was I to complain about our journey in a Chevy Impala with a great suspension system and which never failed us once throughout the eight day long journey. I asked for God's help in locating an apartment for us so that our next obstacle could be overcome, and we could start to settle in our new adventure together.

The next day we drove into Los Angeles and located the law school campus which was in the Hancock Park area of the city, a very nice neighborhood. The personnel at the law school provided us with some ideas of where we might look for an apartment near the law school. Being a relatively new law school with a heretofore mostly local student body, the administration had not yet developed the community resources to assist out-of-state students with housing referrals. We traveled a few miles to Hollywood where someone suggested we might find someplace to live. We spent a very long and discouraging day apartment hunting. Everything seemed either too expensive or too rundown. We returned to our motel room and Victoria burst into tears. "This is not looking good, Martha. What have we gotten ourselves into?" she sobbed.

Being the rescuer I was in those days, I took her in my arms and told her it would be okay - that she should take off the day tomorrow, sleep in, have a late breakfast at the restaurant next door, and I would venture back into the city to look some more. And so I did. With the L.A. Times in hand I went apartment shopping. Within a couple hours I had located a decent apartment in Hollywood for $200 a month, and told the manager I had a roommate I would bring back to look at the premises. The apartment was a relatively large one bedroom apartment, with a master bedroom, large bathroom, family room which overlooked a very nice palm laden courtyard, and a decent sized kitchen.

I went back to the motel and got Victoria. She perked up a good bit when I told her what I had found. We headed back to the location and the apartment manager said he needed to have some type of credit references since he knew we were from out of state and could not accept out of state checks. Victoria pulled out her Master Card, and in 1979 that was all that manager needed to see to believe we were a good credit risk. He had encountered difficulty himself trying to get a Master Card so he knew we must have resources. We wrote a check for the first and last months rent, plus a modest security deposit.

The next couple of days we went out and ordered some cheap furniture for our apartment, which we charged for future payment. We went to the Department of Motor Vehicles for our California licenses, opened bank accounts and bought kitchen utensils. We went back to the law school, purchased our books for the first semester courses - torts, legal bibliography and writing, criminal law, and a course in legal analysis. We were settled in, or so I thought. Nothing could prepare me for the educational experience of a lifetime. I had never been exposed to education by confrontation. It is euphemistically referred to as the Socratic method of learning. In the weeks and months ahead, I would understand why Socrates' students insisted he drink poison!

Learning to think like a lawyer was an extremely painful experience for me. I had done well in my academic pursuits heretofore by learning to absorb masses of information, synthesize ideas into term papers and theses too numerous to mention. I had always found writing, whatever the subject, a task I could master. The classroom up to this point had been a place where ideas were merely brain-stormed, or facts were learned. None of this had prepared me for the law school classroom where one was to question whether the facts were really the facts, and bantering about intellectual ideas was valued somewhat below wood shop 101 in the care and tending of future lawyers.

The classroom in most every law school until very recently was a place where you became humiliated at your ignorance, although you may well have spent twelve to fifteen hours studying the one assignment being discussed. The professor, employing what is called the case study method of teaching (aka the "Socratic method"), asks you to identify the issue or issues at play in each case. Additionally, you are to pick out the salient facts upon which the court's decision turned, and the rationale employed by the court in reaching its decision. For law school novices, this is no little task. What must be learned is how to analyze problems, seeing both sides of the issue or issues presented. This is critical thinking.

My first law school professor, who succeeded in embarrassing me during my very first class, taught us that law school would essentially teach us two skills - how to research the law, and how to think. I remember coming home after my first night at law school, tossing and turning and finally awakening Victoria. "I can't do this," I told her. "I just can't go back into that classroom again and await my time to be chosen as a sacrificial lamb again."

"Of course you can, and will," replied Victoria with a taint of annoyance that comes with being awakened from sleep. "Do you suppose you are the only one who feels like that? Don't be so egotistical. We're all in the same boat and it is the Titanic. You were the fool tonight. Tomorrow night it will probably be me, and the next night someone else. No one is spared in the process. Look upon it as equal opportunity torment. You've been through worse, don't forget it."

She was right. I'd find a way to survive this experience. Who was I to have thought law school would be an escape from the trauma I'd experience in my ministerial career? At least law school in California, with nearly 40 percent of the class being women in1979, seemed light years ahead of what I'd experienced in seminary and in my professional role as a pastor, where women were largely tokens and conversation pieces.

Victoria would be a tremendous source of support throughout law school. Perhaps because she had attended a women's college on an undergraduate level, where small classrooms meant regular one-on-one debates between professor and student, she never seem ruffled by the law professors questions. She was analytically brilliant as well. I did not have the same level of confidence as she, but I promised myself I would, at a minimum, always be prepared for class by reading the assignments and show the professor I had at least studied the cases.

While Victoria found a day job well ahead of me, I spent my days reading and briefing cases for both of us. I would type out the briefs and give them to her after I picked her up from work and made her dinner. She always read all the cases but used my briefs to help her recall what was important during class time. We studied together on the weekends and when the first grades were released at the end of the semester, she was first in the class and I was second. As job demands and eventual Law Review duties eroded some of our study time, we were unable to maintain those lofty positions in our class but we both graduated with good grade point averages, and ironically shared those averages to the hundredth of a point. We helped each other through those long four years of work and study - we were a formidable pair, or so we thought.

As I look back now on our time in law school and its effect upon our relationship, I must honestly admit law school no doubt prolonged our relationship. The never-ending work involved in getting through law school while also working a day job to pay expenses, as well as working as editors on the Law Review, shifted our focus from intimacy. We were, and had always been, good friends to one another, and we were able to understand the tremendous stress being experienced by the other in these four years, so we asked very little from one another emotionally. There was no time or energy for displaying emotions, or so we thought.

Victoria no doubt temporarily discontinued her search for her true sexual orientation, and I blissfully dreamt about the day we would complete this odyssey and achieve some level of financial stability.

When we had our law school diplomas in hand, and had both passed through the next ordeal known as the California Bar Examination, we would begin to ask more from life, and from each other. We would both become unconsciously restless with one another, and our paths would diverge forevermore.

Before that split happened, we both took a position as associate attorneys in a Century City law firm doing insurance defense work. I still have a picture of the door of that office on the 31st floor of that towering edifice overlooking the Pacific Ocean, which listed our names, one after another on the law firm's door. Yes, we started out in the same law firm as well, doing all the litigation work expected of a first year associate. Victoria had first law clerked for that firm in our last year of law school and the managing partner was willing to hire me as well after law school. I worked very hard, of course, but loved the fact I had a desk in a relatively large office which had a floor to ceiling window with a wonderful view of the Pacific Ocean. Our salaries were actually very modest, but after preacher pay, and minimum wage jobs, we thought we had landed on easy street.

This seemed to be a great life - dressing in nice women's business suits - driving off to a nice office everyday with the woman I loved. I began to talk to her about moving out of our crumbling Hollywood apartment and maybe even buying a home together. She was surprisingly reluctant to discuss this possibility.

I will always remember in complete detail the evening my partner of ten and a half years told me she wanted out of our "marriage." It was a Friday night, and after a hard day's work, we agreed to meet at a Westside Los Angeles Italian Restaurant with one of our good friends who was also an attorney. Diana really enjoyed the garlic smell which permeated the whole block and this was one of her favorite restaurants. Victoria had suggested the get-together to see how we all were doing in our respective associates' positions. By this time, Victoria and I worked in different parts of town and agreed to meet at the restaurant instead of meeting at home and driving together. I would later learn how this spoiled part of her strategy for telling me her news.

The dinner was very enjoyable, and all seemed normal. I told Victoria to drive carefully after walking her to her car and said I would see her at home in about half an hour. Once we got to the apartment I proceeded to see our pets were settled for the night and walked into our bedroom. Victoria was already reading and in bed. As I hung up my newly purchased lawyer suit, she began. "Martha, I have something to tell you. I had hoped to tell you earlier in the evening at the restaurant with Diana present. I had expected to talk to her alone for a few minutes before you got to the restaurant, but it didn't work out that way. You got there too promptly, before Diana arrived, and there was no time for me to talk to her alone."

"Well, for goodness sake, Victoria. What was so important that you felt you needed to talk to Diana about before breaking the news to me? We've always been able to talk about anything I thought."

"Martha, I know of no easy way to say this, but I believe it is time for me to explore dating men again. I have this feeling that I have been turning down my feelings for the opposite sex for a long time. Now that we are out of law school and we both have jobs, it's time for me to explore these feelings. I thought I could tell this all to Diana, who is straight, and your best friend next to me; that she'd be able to help me make the request a little less painful." Victoria wasn't crying and didn't even seem to be that sad. Just matter of fact verbiage and she was right out with it.

You could have pushed me over with a feather. I was in complete denial. This was an issue we had struggled with back East, but I thought it was all over. I was unprepared for her demand to leave our relationship. We were now within grasp of collective material success and professional recognition. This was supposed to be the real beginning for us, not an end. I sat on the bed just staring at her and collecting my thoughts until I managed to quietly inquire, "Is there someone else you are seeing now, Victoria?"

"No, Martha, truly I am not involved with anyone. It's just that when I am around some of the male associates at the firm, or some of our male corporate clients, I feel this strange sensation of wanting to be in the heterosexual world. Maybe dating one of them," she continued in a most mater-of-fact tone.

"What about counseling, Victoria? Would you be willing to enter counseling with me and discuss this before you do this?" I was desperately grabbing for any solution I could find.

"No, Martha. I am sure counseling would not help in this matter. I have thought it through for the past six months. I must be free to explore this side of myself. It would be unfair to you to stay in this relationship when I feel something missing in my life," she tried to reason with me.

It was then I fell apart. I raged and screamed as tears began to flow in torrents down my red cheeks. "I can't believe this. I just can't believe this. When do you plan to move out? I mean I can't have you staying here while you come and go with men. Have you thought about that, or are you even so selfish as to want me to watch you move into this life in full view?" I confronted her with my anger.

"No, I will look for another apartment for myself right away. I understand you can't be around while this is happening," Victoria said with some emotion at least.

"You are damn right I cannot be around and in fact I don't even want to be in this apartment with you tonight. I was a fool to overlook your cold-heartedness seven years ago when you just went off with a man, it all blew up, and you came crawling back to your safe haven. You understand that won't ever happen again. You leave this time, and I will never, ever take you back. Do you understand?" I was shouting so loud now I realized the neighbors must be having quite an earful of lesbian drama.

I threw on some jeans and sneakers and went into the living room to sob on the sofa. The cat and dog tried to comfort me but that made me even sadder. I did decide that very night, I would let her go even though I felt it was the end of my life. Victoria felt counseling would not help us and there was little chance she would ever resume life as a lesbian again. Even if that were a possibility, at 34 years of age, I needed no more ambivalence from her. I could not live my life wondering when would be the next time she would want to leave even if we got past this crisis. I wanted to scream at her some more about throwing away ten years of history together - about breaking my heart beyond repair - about betraying the vows we had said to one another in Boston nine years ago. But I didn't. I told her I would stay with some lesbian friends for a few days until she got her affairs in order. With that, I walked out the door, and the next few days, in a complete daze, I tried to sleep on my friends' couch, and keep myself together enough to work. About the time she left our relationship I had secured a new legal position in the eastern area of Los Angeles County so I did not have to see her at work at least where we had been associates together. I would cry all the way to work, pull myself together before I walked into the office, and vanish into my office until 5 p.m. when I would exit not having eaten a thing. I had little appetite for food or life.

It was during this time of devastation that I chose to come out to my parents for the first time. In retrospect I don't know what I was thinking in doing so at that moment, but then let's face it, there is never a good time to come out to your parents if they are the least bit intolerant of having a gay son or lesbian daughter. I am sure I wanted support and love from my parents as I moved through this period of heartbreak. I also knew my parents had liked Victoria. I knew they thought she was very bright with a delightful laugh and that they had always been extremely cordial and pleasant to her. Somehow I held out hope in coming out to them that they would share my hurt and emotionally support me.

But, my parents were Christian fundamentalists and initially love and support was far from what I received. I have totally forgiven, particularly my father, who wanted to lecture me about the Biblical admonitions against homosexuality when I told my parents in a letter about this horrible event of Victoria leaving my life and what the true nature of our relationship had been. My father responded to my coming out letter with a phone call that went something like this: "Martha, we got your letter and we can't say we are totally surprised because when we visited you in California we thought maybe you were involved in a sexual relationship with Victoria. But you must understand that the Bible is very clear about this. Victoria has chosen the right thing here, and we hope you will come to understand you need to turn your back on this and follow her example."

I was, of course, furious and deeply hurt. I remember my exact response: "Dad, at 34 years of age and a seminary education, I need no lectures from you about Biblical literalism." I slammed the phone down on the receiver. It was the only time in my entire life that I ever hung up the phone on my father. How dare he lecture me about this when I was hurting so. A few days later I received a letter from my mother which was much more conciliatory. She said she did not feel about this issue exactly as my father and that if one thing should be followed from Christ's teachings, it was to "judge not lest ye be judged." I was thankful for this letter from my mother for I saw some chance to stay in contact with them and work through this in the months and years ahead. The final story about my parent's thoughts on my homosexuality can best be summed up as a quiet acceptance of me within the context of "judge not lest ye be judged." We did not talk much about homosexuality because it made them very uncomfortable and I was not willing to invest all the energy it would take to help rid two Christian fundamentalists of these preconceived notions about homosexuality as an abomination

I do think they did the very best job they could within the theological context from whence they came to accept me and later my new partner. They were always very kind and gentle to my new partner and always regaled her with birthday and Christmas gifts. So I thank God for giving me parents who did not turn their backs on me and stretched their world view to accept me as best they could.

For those of you who read this book and have not yet come out to your parents I can only say it is the old phrase of "short-term pain for long-term gain." Whatever your parents reaction may be, in the long term you will feel a huge weight lifted off your conscience when you stop trying to be someone you are not. As I said in the first few pages of this book, nothing is more important than the integrity of the soul - everything must be sacrificed for that integrity - even the possible love and support of the people who are very important in your life. The real test of their love will be when they know you are gay. How will they react in the long run? Give your family time to absorb the awareness of your sexual orientation and pray for their awakening to the understanding God loves you no less than they, and that God made you just the way you are - you are surely as much part of God's creation as they.

I have been very blessed to have wonderful heterosexual friends over the decades who never blinked an eye or changed their friendship with me when I came out to them. Either I have had extraordinary talent in picking good friends or God put all these wonderful people in my life to make life a little easier. I think it is a combination of both those factors. As for coming out to friends, if they don't take it well, it would be my opinion they are not people who deserve to be in your life and God will replace them with more understanding friends in the years ahead. We must trust God to supply all our needs and that includes good friends.

After Victoria moved out, we had very little contact. I was able to reach her at her new apartment on a Saturday afternoon in the fall of 1984 and arranged to have lunch with her. I had moved on to new employment as previously indicated and never saw her through work connections. I had no intention of resuming our relationship that Saturday afternoon. I had already met another wonderful woman and knew my life would be with her. I just thought a better ending had to be possible for us. She made a fabulous lunch and we talked for about an hour. She was dating someone but made it very clear she did not want to talk about who it was. I would later learn from another source, it was a male associate at the office who was in the process of getting a divorce from his wife. When it was time for me to leave, and go on to my new life partner, we embraced, and her embrace was warm and genuine. I looked into her eyes and told her I would never forget her. And then, I was gone from her life and would never see her again.

About four years later Victoria's sister wrote me a note to inform me that Victoria had married an engineer who lived in Long Beach. Victoria had abruptly ended all contact with me a couple years before this and now I knew why. No doubt she feared her husband and his conservative family would not approve of her past. This was the ultimate betrayal I thought. "For God's sake," I told myself. "I am a good woman - an accomplished person in my own right. What is she so ashamed of that she doesn't even want to talk to me on the telephone from time to time." This rejection tore me apart for many years, even as I moved into a wonderful new relationship with a woman who was sure of her lesbianism and had never a thought of infidelity.

I did have one last telephone conversation with Victoria. Her parents were coming to California for a first visit with her and her husband of a year. Victoria's father had not been well and her sister wondered if I might be able to meet with her and the parents for dinner. I told her sister that I wanted this to be okay with Victoria because I knew this was the first Christmas she was entertaining her family with her husband. I would get back to her and let her know what we could arrange.

The next Monday I telephoned what I knew to be Victoria's last working address. The receptionist who answered the phone did not seem to know anyone there by the name of Victoria. After a few minutes the receptionist and I were able to establish that Victoria was there, but had totally changed her first and last name when she married. She put me on hold and the next voice I heard was Victoria's warm laugh and hello.

"Well, that was awkward," I commented. "I had no idea you had changed your first name too. When the receptionist suggested I might want to speak to you with this new name, I was very confused."

"I am sure you were. I changed my first name because Jon didn't like it and preferred my middle name. So I just took my middle name as my first and of course his last name," she replied with seemingly little discomfort. I couldn't take all this in. A woman I had met through the feminist movement had not only taken his name, which was alright by me, but to change her first name just because he didn't like it!

"Look, I won't hold you up. I am very sure you are very busy there at the firm. Your sister called to say she and your parents were going to be out for Christmas and they wanted to know if they could get together with me somewhere for dinner. I didn't give your sister a reply yet because I wanted to make sure it was okay for me to see them, this being their first Christmas with you and all." I used a most matter of fact tone and awaited her reply.

"Well, I don't know," she replied and then I could hear her sobbing on the other end of the phone.

"Does Jon know anything about us, Victoria?"

"He knows more than most. We never talk about it," she choked out her reply through more sobs.

"I get the picture," I said in a very cold voice. "You need to say no more. It is obvious the prospect of my meeting your parents on this trip even outside the presence of you and Jon is not something with which you are comfortable, so I will tell your sister that I can't meet them. Please be assured you will never hear from me again." I hung up the phone with authority, sat back in my office chair and cried through feelings of anger and rejection.

When her family arrived for the visit, her sister phoned me again and begged me to meet with her and her parents. But I told her sister I was firm about not meeting with them because the prospect was so disturbing to Victoria, and I did not want to intrude upon an important family occasion, even in private, for one dinner. I told her sister how shocked I was that Victoria had changed her first name and she agreed her family was still trying to get used to it. I will never know if I did the right thing in rejecting that invitation to have dinner with Victoria's sister and parents. It would have been the last time I could have seen Victoria's father for he was very sick and died a few years later. Her Dad had always been very accepting of our relationship and told Victoria how wonderful he thought it was that I loved her so much. I am sorry I never got to give him a last hug.

It was in late November 1997 when the phone rang in my courtroom late one afternoon. My bailiff informed me that Victoria's sister was calling me and that it was an emergency. I hurried into chambers and picked up the phone. "Well, hi, sis, this is Marti. What's up? Are you and your Mom okay?"

"Marti, it's about Victoria; she's been killed."

It took me several seconds to catch my breath and gather my wits. "My God, sis, when was this and what happened to her?"

"Well, it was just two nights ago. Apparently she and Jon were driving back from some type of English car road rally outside Los Angeles, and their car went over a cliff. Jon was killed instantly. Victoria was airlifted to a nearby hospital where she died a few hours later. I couldn't get there in time, of course."

"I just can't believe it. She was just 47 years old. What an incredible loss for you. I know how close you were to her. How is your Mom taking it?"

"Well, Mom's trying to cope as best she can having just recently lost Dad and now her oldest child. But she is a strong woman and she will no doubt make it through. I was just wondering if you knew of some of Victoria's favorite hymns or poetry we might use during a memorial service. We are planning a service for the West Coast and also one on the East Coast at Martha's Vineyard where they often traveled and Jon had a family compound there. She wanted to be cremated with her ashes strewn in the ocean there."

"I am sure I can come up with some suggestions for songs and poems but not at this minute. I'll have to call you back within a day if that is alright with you," I spoke these last two lines with a very broken voice and I knew I was about to burst into tears. "You know I loved your sister very much."

"Marti, yes, I know how much you loved her. I can certainly wait a day or two to hear back from you." She then gave me her telephone number and I hung up the phone in disbelief. It was a fait accompli. I would never see Victoria again. I had hoped for that one last conversation where we sat down over a cup of tea with many years elapsed, thanking each other for our importance to each other's life. Victoria was my first true love, and first love is very powerful as anyone knows, gay or straight. We often attach more importance to it than we should and sometimes try to unfairly measure our subsequent loves to the standard of emotion we felt when we met our first love. This is not what God intended for us. I now understand that to be at peace with life, one must see the growth that occurred with every tragedy or what seemed to be a bad ending in our life. Without these endings and unwanted tragedies we would never move on to what will usually become more understanding and actualization of our purpose on earth.

After this experience with Victoria I understand there are truly bisexual people in our world. I have some lesbian friends who say being a bisexual is just a failure to make a choice and that you are either gay or straight. I believe that we all fall somewhere on a scale of exclusively homosexual to exclusively heterosexual, and that some people end up right in the middle of that scale with distinct interests in both sexes. I think Victoria was one of those people, and being from a conservative Southern environment, it was more comfortable for her to act on her heterosexuality than to remain in a lesbian world where you are often despised by those who are not gay, and certainly your chances of professional and social advancement are limited.

Did she love me? Of that I have no doubt. I just need to read her letter of Valentine's Day 1976 and I am assured of her love. As I write this book, I understand her purpose in my life and am thankful to God that she was in my life for over ten years. She rests with the angels now, and the hurt I once felt has been given over to God in exchange for a measure of peace that the relationship had to happen, and I had to move on to become who I am.

CHAPTER FIVE

A Door Closes - A Window Opens

All of us have a year in our life when we can say that life took a decided change of course. Often, as we resist this transition, we can see little good in the change and wonder why God is putting us through this pain. My first experience like this was the year I left the ministry and was unsure if Victoria would follow me in that decision. That year I wandered about, searching for a new career, and facing the possibility of losing Victoria forever. But 1984 was also such a year, the year Victoria left my life forever, I met my life partner, Pam, and I secured my most meaningful attorney position which would propel me onto the bench.

Just as Victoria was leaving me, I began to experience an onset of high blood pressure. I had never battled this condition before. No doubt the extreme stress of my loss of Victoria exacerbated the situation, causing me to seek medical attention. Again, but for this initial bout with high blood pressure I would never have met my life partner, now of 26 years.

As part of my medical attention to this problem, the doctor sent me for a chest x-ray to make certain I did not have an enlarged heart. It was then I met Pam, a very attractive and personable x-ray technologist. Over the next few weeks we would run into each other at the clinic when I went in for my weekly blood pressure checks. Within short order, after a diet regimen prescribed by my doctor, my blood pressure was back to normal, and I had a first date arranged with Pam.

Most of our friends cautioned both of us to go slow in this dating process. Her friends warned her I was no doubt on the rebound and anything we shared in the process would be temporal to say the least. My friends were happy I had met someone so nice and so cute so quickly but said I should introduce her to all my friends before I made any decisions about making our relationship more permanent. One other complicating factor was that Pam's family had watched her go through a wretched court battle with her former partner over their jointly owned home, and neither her mother or sisters wanted to see her go through that again. Maybe hearing I was a lawyer gave them even more cause for concern!

While all this advice was certainly sound, we were very much attracted to one another - not only the "chemical" attraction we all seek in a partner - but we fully respected each other as decent human beings, having similar values and goals in life. Pam had put herself through two years of college and her x-ray program. She was, and remains to this day, a good money manager, and when I met her in 1984 she owned her own home. She was an accomplished guitar player who had spent several years playing at folk masses in the Catholic Church. I, too, had used my guitar playing abilities in my ministry and on our first date at her home, we truly did make music together playing her beautiful Martin and Gibson guitars for hours.

I would learn that first night she had prepared for the religious life at a convent in Iowa and had desired to spend her life as a nun but for a very controlling and overly zealous mother superior who made her question her vows of obedience. So she did not stay in the religious life long and returned to California where she took up her new occupation in x-ray. She told me that when she had met me that very first day she thought I was possibly a nun - conservatively dressed in a brown suit but with a very open and friendly disposition. To this day, we both believe that God brought our lives together and it is this belief that has kept us together even in our difficult times together.

In these first few weeks of our relationship, we expressed to one another the desire to be life partners. I moved into Pam's home and we began the blissful time together which all couples enjoy those first few months together. We instantly recognized that we each had some very different abilities from one another which lead to a comfortable mix of household duties and responsibilities. We were both working so chores were shared. Pam is one of those truly unique individuals who has the mechanical sense to fix anything or make anything. Having little or none of that talent, I marveled at these capabilities. But more important still was the fact that she "fixed my heart." Knowing I would grieve the loss of Victoria for sometime, Pam was quite patient as I went about that grief process, with the self-assurance that she had something better to offer me in our life together. On the heels of having felt as if I had lost everything when Victoria left, I found the safe harbor of her home and heart - a place where I could emotionally regroup and heal.

With Pam's encouragement, that same year I made a transition from my dead end position as an assistant legal counsel for three school districts to that of a deputy district attorney for Los Angeles County. In my position as assistant legal counsel I would never have any meaningful courtroom experience. I applied for the deputy district attorney job even though I thought I probably would not get hired given the tremendous competition for such a position.

Many attorneys want to work for the Los Angeles District Attorney's

Office which is the largest prosecutorial agency in the United States, but few are chosen. God looked down upon me again, and guided me on a path which would lead to much professional fulfillment, and eventually to the location of my new vocation, the bench. God had worked this miracle by providing me with a partner who believed I was capable of doing whatever I wanted in the legal profession.

Many asked me during those years as a prosecutor how I reconciled being a Christian minister with my new role as a "persecutor" of those who committed crimes. It seemed so inconsistent to them that a religion which preached forgiveness could be an active part of someone's life who spent their working days pursuing judgments against criminals. I think many well-meaning Christians often confuse the concepts of justice and forgiveness. Many Christians believe that true forgiveness means not holding people accountable for the consequences of their criminal behavior. I do not believe God equates the two concepts of forgiving and forgetting the consequences. We should not be merciless in extracting punishment for immoral and criminal behavior, neither should we ignore the healing which can take place for the individual who has wronged his or her community and is now confronted with the consequences.

Christ certainly understood this difference when he was on the cross surrounded by two criminals. One of the criminals was bitter and not the least remorseful for what he had done. The other criminal understood that he had done wrong and deserved punishment, but that Jesus' execution was not right and that Jesus was innocent of any wrongdoing. Christ assured this remorseful criminal that he would join God that day in eternal life. Christ could have delivered this criminal miraculously from his suffering on the cross but he did not. Christ gave the remorseful criminal something better, eternal life.

I always felt comfortable standing before a jury and pleading for a conviction because as a deputy district attorney I was fortunate enough to have supervisors who never forced me to take a matter to trial with charges I did not believe I could be proved beyond a reasonable doubt. I understand my experiences in this regard may have been unique and that there are prosecutors and prosecutorial agencies which pursue underhanded means of gaining convictions against criminal defendants. As a judge I have seen a few prosecutors in my courtrooms over the past 19 years who have not always turned over all the exculpatory evidence to defense counsel or who have somehow not represented the whole truth of a matter. But, whether it was God looking out for me in this role, or I was just lucky, I never had to compromise my principles to pursue a case or win a conviction.

After some significant experiences trying cases, I was fortunate to gain a position with the Appellate Division of the District Attorney's Office. Here, I pursued appeals on behalf of the People as well as responded to appeals brought by defendants. A whole new skill of legal writing was honed for me at that time, and I even had the opportunity to pursue a case on behalf of the People all the way to the United States Supreme Court, filing an amicus brief in the case of Payne v. Tennessee, which allowed for family members of homicide victims to give victim impact statements at death penalty sentencing proceedings.

I realize I was blessed to have this very positive experience as a prosecutor, and as mentioned above, not every prosecutor or prosecutorial agency is highly ethical and fair-minded. It is my belief that miscarriages of justice most frequently occur in our criminal justice system when winning a conviction becomes the only goal of a prosecutor, allowing a prosecutor to remain blind to even the most overwhelming evidence of the defendant's innocence. When doing justice becomes a secondary consideration to winning cases, the justice system fails miserably. Unfortunately I have known a few prosecutors, and had one or two appear before me as I was sitting on the bench, who were more invested in winning a case than looking clearly at the facts which might give rise to the defendant's innocence. When a judge discovers a prosecutor has done this just once, that prosecutor's reputation is ruined forever, and rightly so.

There is no doubt that my theological background, as well as my parents' insistence upon honesty at all costs, kept me respectful of the truth as well as instilled in me the need to search for the truth. It was the very fact that Christianity was not about winning, but was rather about a journey towards truth that helped me resist any temptations to take unfair advantage of an adversary or defendant. There is no doubt that the People's attorney can marshal great resources against indigent defendants and succeed in covering up the truth about a particular case, perhaps forever. But when you believe that you may one day be held accountable by a greater judge than the one who sits behind a wooden bench, the desire to improperly employ these resources evaporates.

I felt good about myself as an attorney during those years as a prosecutor. The numerous jury trials allowed me to utilize the oratory skills I had fine-tuned at Syracuse University and Princeton, while learning the rules of evidence, so essential to being a good advocate in court. I took my lumps, lost cases I should have won but for my inexperience. I tried to learn to let go of the losses, even accepting that some of them were most likely necessary in the course of justice. This legal experience was a microcosm of my larger life experience - learning to let go of the losses, and accepting that all of them were necessary in the course of my spiritual growth.

The greatest tribute I received as a prosecutor came one day in the midst of a heated courtroom battle. After the evidence had all been presented at a court trial (a trial where the judge is the fact-finder and decides whether or not the defendant committed the crime) the criminal defense attorney launched into a vicious attack upon my integrity as a prosecutor, accusing me of shading the truth and presenting an incomplete case against his client.

The judge before whom I was appearing in this case had not always been my favorite judge. He was often prone to highly sexist comments in open court, and seemed to particularly enjoy chewing up, and spitting out, most prosecutors. I have to admit I was taken by surprise when my adversary began this assault upon my character, and rather than bounding to my feet and screaming back, I sat glued in my seat aghast that my colleague on the other side of counsel table was doing this. He had gotten but a few sentences into his attack when the scowling judge shouted at the top of his lungs, "Enough, Mr. Smith, enough. I may not be certain of just how all of the facts of this case came down but of one thing I am certain. I have had Ms. Bellinger in front of me long enough to know that when she tells you something, you can take it to the bank and deposit it." If I never again hear a word of praise about my conduct in the legal profession, this is all I ever needed to hear - that one judge had come to learn my word was gold.

Within four years of becoming a deputy district attorney I also secured an adjunct professorship in criminal law at La Verne University College of Law. This would become an 18 year association where I also taught a course entitled "Children and the Law,' and developed a third course entitled "Religion and the Law," with both course offerings becoming popular electives at the school. This time as an adjunct professor gave me a chance to have a positive effect upon a new generation of attorneys and share with them some of the real life experiences I had as a deputy district attorney and subsequently a judge.

Although it was hard work having this extra position, I grew as a person and scholar in the area of criminal law and juvenile law, publishing many articles in legal periodicals and eventually co-authoring a bench book on juvenile law which is utilized throughout California. It has been my pleasure to see many of my former law students appear before me in my courtroom once they became attorneys. I never hid my sexual orientation from them but did not make it a cause celebre either. In my quiet way, I believe I changed many students' ideas about what a gay or lesbian professor, attorney, and judge had to offer the legal world and humanity in general. It certainly made for interesting class conversations in the area of Religion and the Law, particularly for the students who struggled with fundamentalistic Christian beliefs in a very pluralistic society.

In my duties as an adjunct law professor I tried to emphasize that one cannot be a good lawyer without being honest. Oh, perhaps in the short run, a slight misrepresentation here and there can cause a courtroom win, and momentarily propel a legal career to new heights. But I have never yet known of a legal career that can be sustained by deceit, nor a soul that can assume the role of a deceiver, and rest in peace either in this world or the next. All the lawyer jokes you have heard - many of them well deserved - have been generated by this belief that winning is everything, and it doesn't matter how you play the game.

From my view on the bench, it is still the lawyers who care about having the case presented in a fair and honest matter that establish a level of credibility with me which assures they will win their cases when they should, regardless of the underhanded tactics their adversaries might attempt. But if you purposely misrepresent the status of a case to me as I preside in my courtroom, my trust in you as an honest advocate will never be fully restored. Integrity is everything to me.

As I look back upon my career as an attorney, I realize this experience provided one additional lesson. I needed to learn to stand tall and resolute in the face of great verbal barrages and personal assaults. In short, it toughened my skin, something I needed badly. Throughout my brief years in the ministry, whenever someone would criticize what I was doing, it seemed like an arrow to my heart. I was so in need of approval and acceptance, that criticism, even when unjustly hurled, would have a way of discouraging me from continuing the task at hand.

Through the law, I learned to listen closely to my adversaries' cases, to separate out the good arguments from the bad, and to separate out the personal attacks from the truth. I have learned that I am not always right, nor do I always understand the law in all its complexities. If an attorney is truly honest with herself, she is humbled by the vastness of the law, and the elasticity of its parameters. What might have been a correct interpretation of the law in the 19th or 20th century can no longer be applied to modern circumstances and changes.

In these ways, the law had been a paradigm of my larger life. God calls us to listen to our adversaries, but also to apply the Rule of Divine Love in separating out the good positions from the bad. God calls upon us to be strong in the face of great personal assaults upon our character even as we endeavor to do God's will. God wants us to realize that we know very little of the Divine Plan, that we should be humbled by its vastness. And finally, God wants us to know that the Divine Plan is ever evolving, that it is in process, and what was once the experience of one generation can never be the experience of another. Through it all, God is still God, and as inept as we may feel at times, we must always remember that we were created according to God's purpose, and have a destiny to fulfill, regardless of the obstacles put in our path.

CHAPTER SIX

To Sit Where Solomon Sat

I was hard at work writing yet one more appellate brief for the Los Angeles District Attorney's Office late in June 1991, when my telephone rang just before noontime. "Hello, Martha? This is Ricardo Torres, the presiding judge of Los Angeles Superior Court. I'd like to congratulate you upon your election to the Superior Court as a commissioner. The results were just tallied and you won the election. You should be proud of the high esteem the judges of the court appear to hold in your abilities. I'll have you talk to my assistant about arranging your swearing-in ceremony."

As I replaced the telephone receiver, a warm glow spread over me. I sat in my chair for several minutes trying to comprehend how this had all happened so quickly. I thanked God for this new opportunity in my life, and also asked for wisdom and courage to undertake the role of jurist. Quite honestly, I was a bit astonished at this news. Only six weeks before I had undergone an interview process to become a Los Angeles Superior Court Commissioner. In California, being a superior court commissioner is considered a judicial position but defined as a subordinate judicial role. Commissioners are empowered by the elected and appointed judges of the court to handle the extra work these judges cannot handle. Commissioners often labor in the areas of family court, juvenile court, and matters of limited legal jurisdiction such as small claims and traffic. In truth, by stipulation of both attorneys on a case, a commissioner can hear almost any case a judge can hear, and some of our more brilliant commissioners have even sat overseeing death penalty proceedings.

In truth, the difference between commissioners and judges has more to do with prestige and pay than ability or competence. In fact many commissioners are more capable at their jobs than any judge appointed by the Governor or elected by the People could ever be. Commissioners receive slightly less pay than judges and are fully employees of the court, susceptible to removal by the court's judges if incompetence or unethical behavior is exhibited by the commissioner at issue. Becoming a commissioner is a highly competitive process in Los Angeles County. When I applied for the position, my application was one of 186 considered. In order to qualify for the position you must now have ten years of experience as an attorney. After reviewing these 186 applications, a committee of judges of the court referred 30 names to another panel of judges to interview these candidates. From those candidates, 16 names are finally put on a list, and when a commissioner position is open, the list is mailed to all 240-plus judges of the court for election. The candidate garnering the most votes wins the position. No campaigning by or for the commissioners is allowed. In theory, you win or lose on your reputation and merit, or the connections you may have made with the judiciary before the selection process.

In the end, I was in a run-off election with another individual who happened to be a judge's son. Providentially I prevailed. I say providentially because I had no inside political connections with the judges at the time of my election and I was unaware of what my reputation might be among the whole judiciary. My interview had gone well I thought, but I still considered my eventual appointment a long shot. I believe to this day that my selection was the hand of God opening another door of opportunity for me.

On July 22, 1991, in the Presiding Judges chambers and the presence of my life partner Pam, as well as dear colleagues from the District Attorney's Appellate Division, I was sworn into office as a court commissioner for Los Angeles County. I would no longer be an advocate, but rather assume the role of mediator, referee and decision maker in court disputes. I knew my life had dramatically changed once again, but nothing prepared me for just how much change this would be.

My first judicial assignment would be in dependency court. This is the court in which child abuse and neglect proceedings are conducted. These courts must decide whether or not children should be removed from their parents due to abuse and neglect, and if the children are removed from their parents, whether the removal will be temporary or permanent. If the children are removed temporarily, then the court oversees the reunification process, while ordering addiction treatment for the parents if required, parenting classes, or perhaps domestic violence counseling if necessary. The judge orders whatever the parents need to get the issues resolved in their families so they can become fit parents, and social workers oversee this rehabilitation process.

These courts must always balance the rights of the parents with the rights of the children, and somehow miraculously decide "what is in the best interests" of these children. This is a monumental task, and an error in judgment can mean the death of a child if the child is returned too soon to abusive parents or caretakers, or if reunification is denied the child can be lost from the parent's life forever.

It would have been impossible for me to make the decisions I had to make during my time in this branch of the court system if I had not relied upon God and seeing this assignment as a very important segment of my spiritual journey. I reminded myself daily that Christ wanted children to have a special place in his Kingdom and implored each of us to become as children if we wanted to really enter and understand his Kingdom. My colleague next door referred to our work as jurists in this venue as "God's work," and he was certainly correct about that.

To completely understand the difficulty of working in this court system you must know a bit about the sheer numbers of children we are talking about at that time. There were approximately 17 courtrooms in 1991 which exclusively handled dependency proceedings. This was necessary to oversee the approximately 60,000 children who appeared in these courtrooms each year. In 1991, every day my courtroom could count on having no fewer that 30 to50 cases on calendar. With all the children, parents, attorneys, social workers and experts appearing in these cases, I could easily have contact with over 300 people a day, coming and going out of my courtroom. It was emotionally exhausting to say the least, and it was fortunate I was only 41 when I started that assignment because I am not sure now at 60, I could have easily made a transition into that judicial assignment. With little time to address each case, the jurist in charge had the nearly insurmountable task of getting to the truth of the situation quickly while also reflecting some level of concern for each case and all the "players" attached to it.

It is very fair to say that for many, many years, the dependency court system was seen as the stepchild of the courts both inside and outside of Los Angeles County. Many judges hated to be assigned to these courtrooms for a variety of reasons: (1) Many of the cases were so horrible to read about - children being beaten, tortured, and neglected at the hands of the parents - that it was difficult for many jurists to encounter such misery on a daily basis; (2) The caseloads were devastating - too many abused and neglected children, and too few courtrooms to handle the cases - the jurist burned out quickly after just a few months on the bench; (3) If you fancied yourself a real judge, with a brilliant career ahead of you, the last place you wanted to be found was in these very humble surroundings, more fit for social workers than a future Oliver Wendell Holmes.

Because of this reluctancy to serve in dependency court, for years judges were sent to this assignment to punish them for things they did or did not do appropriately in their previous judicial assignment. Accordingly, for years the dependency court was a dumping ground for jurists. Of course, the only ones truly affected by this policy were the children and parents who appeared in some courts where the judge hated his assignment and was just waiting for a chance to move on to a better one.

I think this past policy is a sad commentary upon our society in general. Until the last decade of the 20th century, we have never attached much importance to dedicating one's life to helping children, whatever the vocation. We've woefully underpaid many school teachers who shape their minds, we continue to cut back vital services that directly impact children, and we've created a world in which many children have to rear themselves. It is no wonder that the judicial system has often seen little importance in placing its best resources in dependency court.

While I, too, often marveled at the depravity and cruelty that could be perpetrated against the smallest children and shed more than my fair share of tears over their circumstances, I kept telling myself that if I could positively affect the life of just one child each day, the whole day had been well spent. When a child asked his or her attorney at the end of proceeding if they could go and give the judge a hug, I considered such a moment greater payment than any paycheck I would receive as a jurist. When I participated in proceedings that would lead to a child being adopted by a new set of parents who would surround them with love and attention they had never known, I felt a happiness beyond description.

So those years in dependency court were not dreadful ones for me. In Los Angeles County, most children five years of age or older were brought to all their court proceedings by the social workers. This gave the judge a firsthand look at the life he or she was impacting, and highlighted the importance of each judicial decision made. I sought out churches and individuals who were willing to donate stuffed animals to be given to the children who appeared in my courtroom, so they might leave the courtroom a little less traumatized with something soft and cute to cuddle.

As frequently happens when we become a little too comfortable with our place in life, a new obstacle is interjected in our sublime existence to make us sit up and take notice that life isn't without its complications and unpleasant tasks. That was my experience the night before Thanksgiving 1994. I was just completing a wonderful year in my dependency judicial assignment. I had been blessed that year with a wonderful courtroom staff and highly professional attorneys helping me process our heavy caseload each day. We were busy, but the whole courtroom staff felt like we were engaged in the most important task in life, helping children. There did not appear to be even one person in our midst who didn't feel this commitment, and everyone was willing to put aside petty, interpersonal conflicts in the interest of having an effective, caring courtroom.

Just as I arrived home from court that Wednesday evening in 1994, the telephone rang, and a judge I had known for sometime was at the other end of the telephone line telling me he had been appointed the supervising judge in my judicial district and I was being transferred to family law court in my local district effective January 1995! I tried to be pleasant and not reflect the profound disappointment I was feeling. I wanted to stay with my kids in Children's Court. I didn't want to go to "divorce court" and listen to people fight over children, toasters, houses, cars and child support. I didn't want to have to choose between two bad parents in deciding where to place the children they had chosen to use as pawns in their attempts at revenge and retaliation against one another. As a dependency court judge, I could take children away from parents who were horribly emotionally abusive to their children. I wouldn't have that same ability in family law court, the very name of the court being a contradiction in terms.

The best part of my new assignment was being close to home. I lived only 20 minutes from the courthouse and that meant a great deal to my partner who now could see me a little more often during the day and enabled me to pick up some of the chores around the house. Previously my commute to the Children's Courthouse had been no less than an hour and fifteen minutes each way. There were better ways to use that two and a half hours each day than on a stop and go freeway. Pam's health was beginning to wane as she fought several auto-immune diseases and maintained full-time employment at a very physically demanding health care position. In addition to this blessing of being close to home, the other family law jurist next door to my courtroom was a wonderful man with a keen sense of humor and an equally fine mind for family law. Having Doug next door would be my salvation on more than one occasion. Finally, I had a good courtroom staff who had worked in this area of misery and hostility for years, and knew how to handle the public.

I worked extremely hard in this assignment because I was not an expert in family law and I took some 292 matters under submission in my three years in that position, meaning that I issued 292 written decisions out of this courtroom dealing with everything from difficult custody decisions to how to split the family china. Nights and weekends were often taken up with reading and researching the law I should apply, and writing thoughtful decisions. Again, most jurists run from this assignment as well - they call it "pots and pans." I had one egocentric colleague who enjoyed doing high profile criminal cases tell me, "I don't do pots and pans, nor windows."

My colleague's assessment of what a jurist does in family law court was not only demeaning, but quite frankly untrue. When the custody of children was at issue, the jurist once again must step in and determine what is in their best interests as a custody arrangement between the two parents. Who will rear the children often is completely determinative of how that child will turn out as an adult. I think it no mistake that the Bible premises the most important judicial decision of Solomon upon a custody dispute between two women who claimed to be the child's mother. Solomon knew that by appealing to the higher instincts of the true mother, he would learn who deserved to be the stated parent. I tried to do the same.

As I completed my third year in "divorce court," I had many discussions with God about how I could possibly be serving his purpose in this assignment. Many days I faced as many as 30 divorce cases on calendar - thirty sets of people very angry, hurt, and filled with vengeance, who wanted to make it as miserable for the other party as they possibly could. Occasionally they hire attorneys who take up this same agenda, and you can just imagine how much fun it is to preside over these wars, particularly when their attorneys are throwing as much gasoline on these fires as possible.

The irony of my former family court assignment was that I was as a lesbian woman jurist, sitting in a court that assists heterosexual couples with the divorce process. While I could not at that time marry my partner, nor ask the judicial system to assist me in any divorce process I might have to face, I was apparently qualified to render decisions in these family law matters, and could even perform marriage ceremonies. It was also during this period of time on the bench that a very famous serial murderer who sat on death row in San Quentin, the Nightstalker, Richard Ramirez, was allowed to marry a woman fan who had been writing him while he was incarcerated on death row. I asked myself, what kind of world allows a serial murderer to get married but denies a loving lesbian couple of eleven years the same privilege.

In January 1998, I began an assignment as a delinquency court jurist. This new assignment energized me beyond my greatest dreams. In working with troubled teens I got a unique opportunity few others will ever have to turn a life around from a life of crime and self-destruction to a productive life filled with meaning. Of course, it was impossible to help all the young people who appeared before me. Some young people have been so abused, neglected and misdirected by the time they reach the delinquency courtroom, that they become menacing and dangerous anti-social individuals who have to be separated from society before they take another life, or seriously harm themselves. Still other youth must continue to live in economically depressed and crime ridden neighborhoods where gangs thrive, beckoning to young lives in search of identity and meaning. To be part of some group which demands recognition from the larger community, a group which provides the individual with a sense of self-worth and contribution, is what all young people need. Sometimes a gang is the only place such satisfaction is provided for socially and economically deprived young people.

But every day, at least one young man or woman appeared in my courtroom who had graduated from high school or became sober because I gently but forcefully reminded them they would not get off probation until they accomplished these ends. Without that ultimate control over their lives, which for one reason or another the parent had lost, these little miracles of change and accomplishment would never have occurred. There has been an erroneous perception by many Americans that our teenagers are totally out of control and these children represent the most monstrous generation ever raised. Much of this is based upon media hype over isolated incidents such as the Columbine school murders, horrendous acts of murder by gangs in our major cities, especially Los Angeles and Chicago.

But over the past ten years or so, our federal crime statistics actually point to a diminishment of violent crime among juveniles. Nationwide, there is an approximate rehabilitation rate of 70% for the juveniles who enter the delinquency court system. This is largely the case because teenagers are risk-takers who get themselves in trouble without thinking through the consequences of their acts or the consequences of hanging out with the wrong friends. In the last decade, medical studies of the adolescent brain have revealed that most young people, for example, do not have a fully developed brain until age 25. The last part of their brain to develop is that which has to do with judgment and decision making. In short, most young adults, good or bad, are not in their right minds until they have passed well into their twenties. When shown the error of their ways, many teens can turn things around behaviorally.

God had given me an opportunity in this new judicial assignment to reach out and teach young people the value of education, self-respect, and respect for others - an opportunity I know I could not have in any other walk of life. Not having children of my own, it was my way of giving to the next generation some of the love and concern I had the privilege to experience in my own childhood. I knew for the twelve years I was in this assignment, God had me where I was meant to be. All those years I enjoyed the drive to work each day, and spent countless hours speaking to civic groups about delinquency court matters, and authored many speeches and articles dealing with delinquency law and procedure.

One of the greatest struggles most of us endure is keeping our own ego under control. We are often thinking about where we "should be" in the world instead of closely examining the fact that where we are at present may just be where God intends us to be. While it is important to have a sense of self-worth and pride about what we are doing, it is often the constant need for recognition which drives us from the path God wants us to travel.

Beginning about 1999, I was having one final struggle in this regard. I had served then for seven years as a court commissioner and judge pro tem for the Superior Court, but I wanted the full recognition of a state court judgeship through an appointment by the Governor to that status. While I might well perform the very same duties as I had been assuming as a jurist after such an appointment, I saw this possible advancement as a 15% salary increase and full recognition of my judicial abilities. The political realities of advancement to this status through appointment by the Governor did not favor me, and largely because I had chosen to be "out" as a lesbian jurist. This did not mean that as a commissioner I had placed a nameplate on my bench which stated "Lesbian Jurist," but it did mean I never lied to anyone about my relationship with Pam. To hide in the closet for political advancement was wrong to me. I would never "out" anyone else, nor question their desire to remain in the closet, but as said before, the integrity of my soul was at issue. I know of one lesbian jurist who remained in the closet and got an appointment to the state bench from a former conservative Republican Governor. When people called her house and her partner answered, she would tell these people later that the person who answered the phone was her housekeeper. I do not condemn this woman, I only find it sad that society had brought her to this lie.

During my first eight years on the bench, a Republican Governor,

Pete Wilson, inhabited the State House. He could not be what you would call a friend to the gay community. As politics would have it, some of the time he was Governor he had aspirations of being President. Being perceived as gay friendly would not have helped him one bit, and so he appointed no openly gay or lesbian jurists to the bench during his tenure. Before Governor Wilson we had eight years of Republican George Deukmejian as Governor who also appointed no openly gay or lesbian jurists. For sixteen years, several highly qualified gay and lesbian people were frozen out of the judiciary in California due to a Governor's fear of challenging the state's homophobia. While California might appear to many in the United States as the land of "fruits and nuts," there are some very politically conservative and wealthy forces at work in the state as well, as has been tragically exemplified through the very narrow passage of Proposition 8, outlawing same-sex marriage in November 2008.

While an inner voice nagged at me about not having attained the epitome of my judicial career, another more rational voice told me I am, and have always been, right where God intended. As a court commissioner and judge pro tem I had labored in the humblest vineyards of family law and juvenile law. Most aspiring jurists, as previously pointed out, care little for these assignments because they are not prestigious enough. Handling high profile criminal trials and multi-million dollar civil lawsuits is the goal of most jurists.

In the final analysis, this all gets down to a matter of integrity. Had I hidden my sexual orientation while on the court as a commissioner, I might have been appointed by the Governor to a higher judicial post years ago. As highlighted previously, I knew more than a few closeted jurists who were appointed by the previous Republican governors.

CHAPTER SEVEN

The Window Opens Wider

When Governor Gray Davis swept into office in January 1999, the gay community had high hopes in many regards. They hoped he would be gay friendly, pushing the parameters of gay rights and particularly domestic partnership status to reflect more nearly the status of marriage in California. Of course, the gay legal community wanted Governor Davis to start making some judicial appointments from a large pool of very competent openly gay and lesbian attorneys who had been waiting in the wings as the Republicans ran the state.

Without hesitation, I sent my judicial application to Governor Davis on my 49th birthday, March 1, 1999. This was a tedious process in that a judicial application contains about 60 questions and can take a full fifty typed pages to complete. I went about the usual process of seeking judicial endorsements and assistance in bringing my name to the attention of the Governor's Judicial Appointments Secretary. But I never have been, nor ever will be a very hard-driving political individual. It was so difficult for me to ask people "in the know" to write letters and make phone calls on my behalf for judicial appointment by the Governor.

On top of everything else, one can imagine the huge number of qualified Democratically oriented straight and gay attorneys seeking appointment. The pool was immense. The competition was overwhelming. In Los Angeles County especially, a county containing one third of all the jurists in the State of California, the pool of applicants included some of the finest litigators and legal advocates in the country. Governor Davis made some very fine appointments to well-deserved individuals, some of them were my fellow commissioners. I watched him appoint three openly gay men to the bench in Los Angeles County, but no lesbians.

After four years, my judicial application took some notice and my name was submitted to the State Bar and County Bar for evaluation. This process essentially involves both entities mailing out several hundred evaluation forms to attorneys and judges who know you, asking them to evaluate your intelligence, legal knowledge, demeanor and ethics among other categories. Both the State Bar and County Bar conduct independent evaluations, and once they have gathered all these forms you are interviewed by each group. You are confronted with any negative things people have said about you and given a chance to respond. All the respondents to the evaluation forms are guaranteed absolute confidentiality, so you will never be told who made any of these negative comments, if any, against you. It can be a very frightening process.

I suppose because I had faced so much professional adversity in my life during my ministerial career, and further toughened by the rigors of being a courtroom prosecutor, God had brought me to this process with a little less fear than most. I knew God would love me no matter what when I walked into the interview room, and when I walked out.

My favorite chapter of the Bible, Romans 8 says in verse 31, "If God is for us, who can be against us?" What did I have to fear?

Both interviews went extremely well and remarkably no negative evaluations were submitted against me by the fellow jurists and attorneys with whom I had worked. The County Bar evaluation process was actually an uplifting experience because among the committee members evaluating me was a distinguished lesbian litigator who, like I, had been with her partner for sometime, and as a couple, they had recently been refused baptism of their son by the local Roman Catholic parish. The fact that I was a lesbian came out when one of the interviewing attorneys asked me why I had left the ministry and turned to the law. I simply told the interviewing committee the truth, and with that came a connection with that committee which was immeasurable. Surely God's hand was all in this, I believed.

Within a month, the Governor's Appointments Advisor called my courtroom and asked for an interview, and that does not happen unless favorable reports are given from the State Bar and the County Bar Associations. This interview with the Judicial Appointments Advisor in August 2003 also seemed to go well. Unfortunately, Governor Davis was the first Governor in the history of the State of California to be recalled that Fall and the last few judicial appointments he made were to other individuals who had been waiting in line ahead of me.

To say I was a little heartbroken about this turn of events doesn't come close to my dismay. Why had God even led me down this dead end road? Maybe God wanted me to be humbled - maybe my ego and the prestige of this judgeship had overshadowed the larger mission of my life - to help the forgotten. Obviously, I could do this as a court commissioner - less money, less opportunity to change the court system for the better - but essentially the same job I would have had as a state court judge.

I didn't let myself remain sad for long. My partner had been rooting for me from the sidelines my whole career and knew my disappointment. But she re-emphasized to me in our quiet moments together that she loved me no less as a commissioner than if I had been appointed a judge by the Governor. "Maybe you can retire sooner, honey, and I'd get to spend more time with you." And so, I set a tentative date for retirement at 59, and moved on.

Many of my colleagues on the bench were also sad for me. They knew how much time and energy I had put into the court system. They knew my fifteen years as an adjunct law professor and service to the education of fellow delinquency court judges, commissioners and referees made me a deserving candidate for advancement in the judiciary. They expressed their sadness to me. Interestingly most all of these dear colleagues were Republicans with little or no homophobia.

I had completely given up the expectation of being further elevated within the court system. I was at peace with the decision of continuing on as a court commissioner, presiding over delinquency cases for about another two or three years when I would retire from the bench and move on to some other phase of life. I believed God had me working where he wanted me to be. This was about me learning to let go of my ego and to remember one of the most important lessons Christ taught: "Inasmuch as you do this for one of the least of my brethren, you do it for me."

So I was astounded when upon answering the phone in my chambers early one morning in September 2004, I heard the voice of a long-time judicial acquaintance encouraging me to send in a judicial application to Governor Arnold Swartzennegger for elevation to a state court judgeship. I told my friend I didn't think it likely a Republican Governor would want a life-long lesbian Democrat as one of his judicial appointments.

"I think you are wrong about that, Martha. This Governor is not going to do politics as usual in his judicial appointments. He is looking for highly qualified individuals in their fifties and from what I hear you fit the bill. I am one of the Governor's inside advisors on judicial appointments and I think I can get you through the first hurdle of being recommended for State and County Bar evaluation. Then, it is up to you from there on in."

I thanked my friend and told him I'd mull it over for 24 hours. And I did. I had many talks with God and my partner, Pam. She, of course, was behind me 100 percent. So, once again, I put together a well organized and attractive judicial application, attaching an appellate brief I had filed with the United States Supreme Court as an appellate attorney, along with some of my published legal periodicals on delinquency law. Within weeks I was being interviewed once again by the State and County Bar associations for their stamp of approval, and on April 13, 2005, the call came from the Governor's Office for me to fly to Sacramento for an interview with the Appointments Advisor, Mr. John Davies. I had heard rumors in the past that he might have been homophobic when he served as Governor Wilson's Judicial Appointments Secretary in the 1990's. But I later realized that he was no doubt under marching orders from Governor Wilson to weed out gay candidates. Mr. Davies had no such marching orders from Governor Swartzennegger in 2005, and I found Mr. Davies brilliant, knowledgeable in all areas of the law, and quite charming. The one time I mentioned my partner in the interview he seemed not the least bit uncomfortable.

To make a long story short, my application was processed with warp speed through the Governor's Office, and on June 13, 2005, I was appointed to the Superior Court of the State of California for the County of Los Angeles. What was ironic about my appointment on June 13, was that it was the same day I was having exploratory surgery that turned out to be a four hour hysterectomy due to ovarian cancer. As my partner waited in the hospital waiting room, she knew a 45 minute exploratory surgery as billed must have turned into something more significant and ominous. When the surgeon appeared, she told Pam not to worry, I was okay, but that it appeared I had stage one ovarian cancer and hopefully all the biopsies she had taken in the surrounding areas would turn out to be negative. They did read out as being negative for more cancer. The cancer had been encapsulated and had not spread. Even chemotherapy would not be needed.

At a time when I would normally be lifting a glass of champagne in celebration of my appointment with all my colleagues and life partner, I was lying in a hospital bed with a morphine drip trying to figure what this was all about - a judicial advancement and cancer all at once? I was not angry or particularly frightened by the cancer my surgeon had found, I was just puzzled. I finally resolved that God had spared me to continue to work for his children even more from a more powerful position which could effect real change to children in the legal system. Within eighteen months, I was asked to serve as the supervising judge of the delinquency courts in the Eastern District of Los Angeles County.

CHAPTER EIGHT

Searching For A Church Home

When I left the parish ministry in 1977, I did not leave spirituality behind. I only knew I would need to find a church home that would accept me for what I was - a lesbian Christian. This search would take years to complete, and would lead me, as a visitor, in and out of numerous denominations. Even today, I cannot truthfully say the church I attend, as open and friendly as it may be, is the major vehicle for my spiritual enrichment. Sometimes in the quiet of my home library as I read various progressive Christian writers as Henri Nouwen, or read the works of the Dalai Lama, I feel a greater connection to God than when I am worshiping in church.

The summer I left my pastorate and went to Harvard Divinity for post graduate studies, I attended the Quaker meeting in Cambridge for several weeks. For those unfamiliar with Quakerism, the "silent meeting" is a form of worship where Quakers would gather and sit quietly until one of the members was inspired by the Spirit of God to make some reflection upon the world or community which would enrich the souls of the gathered. I had also come to realize that Quakers were more open to gay and lesbian individuals becoming part of their community. This obviously encouraged me to explore further.

Perhaps because my soul was so restless and my spiritual energy very scattered at the time, I was unable to fully appreciate the beauty of the "silent meeting." But I was also a bit offended by a discussion group leader one evening at the Quaker meeting house who proclaimed that he was a birthright Quaker as contrasted to the numerous converts to their religion. The hubris expressed that evening made me ponder whether I would be relegated to second class citizenship within that religious community were I to join. Now that I look back upon that man who was so proud of his birthright Quakerism and think about the Quakers who were hung on the Boston Common for their faith in pre-colonial times, maybe I understand his pride a little better, misplaced as it might have been.

My next church visitation occurred when I moved to Florida in the winter of 1977 and attended a relatively new United Church of Christ church in Tampa. While finishing my theological education at Boston University School of Theology, I was aware that the United Church of Christ had just ordained its first openly gay pastor - Bill Johnson - and I held out hope that the UCC would be a more open church to gay and lesbian people. Of course this was Florida in 1977, the home state of Anita Bryant who was one of the early spokespersons for late twentieth century homophobia, and so who was I kidding when it came to acceptance? I remained in the closet, and ended up being a shoulder upon which to cry for the young pastor of this congregation whose wife was divorcing him because she could not take the demands of being a pastor's wife. I sympathized with her struggle, too, of course.

When I moved back to Upstate New York in early 1978 to be with Victoria, we tried out several churches - United Methodist, UCC, Lutheran, Presbyterian. But none were open to receiving gay or lesbian persons unless your sexual orientation was kept secret. It will always remain a source of amazement for me that we were able to walk in and out of several churches without having even one person say hello to us.

After we moved to California, we briefly attended a Quaker silent meeting in South Central Los Angeles. Curiously, as is often the case in the melting pot which is Southern California, that Quaker meeting took on the flavor of the Korean community nearby. Only one other Caucasian woman attended this meeting with Victoria and I. The leader of the meeting was a middle-aged Korean man. It was curious to both Victoria and I that the Korean women never seemed to speak at these silent meetings. Later, when we began to understand the patriarchal nature of the Korean community, we understood why the Korean women remained silent. Victoria and I chose not to make our lesbianism an issue at this meeting. Chances are that our intuition that such an orientation would not be welcome there was very well true. We did not attend for long.

We also attended two different Metropolitan Community Churches - a church founded by Rev. Troy Perry, a gay Pentecostal, for gay and lesbian individuals who needed a church home. While it was wonderful to take communion together as an open couple and be able to hold hands during the service, the Pentecostal flavor of these particular congregations was not an easy fit for either of us. We also did not really enjoy being separated completely from the straight community. During our time in law school, Victoria and I had developed many heterosexual friends with whom we were open about our relationship. It was the "real" world to have both gay and straight friends as well as gay and straight fellow workers. Why should we be separate in our experience of worship, even if most of the world preferred it that way?

For the most part, we did not attend church on Sundays during our law school years. We used those mornings to sleep in, leisurely read the newspaper, and begin our legal studies for the week ahead. I felt little guilt about being away from the larger church in those days, a church which with few exceptions, had no place for me or my partner.

Right after Victoria left my life, I attended briefly a third Metropolitan Community Church in the San Fernando Valley. I will always be thankful for the pastoral counseling of the minister who listened to my sobs and cries over the end of my relationship with Victoria and for a gay couple in that church who surrounded me with their love and understanding during this time.

When Pam and I became partners, we recognized our mutual desires for spirituality but we came from very different traditions. Endowed with firm Roman Catholic beliefs but disenchanted with her church's stand on many issues, Pam was not attending Mass on a regular basis when I met her. I did not push my Protestantism on her either, but from time to time we would go to Mass together, and I was eager to learn more about her religious tradition beyond what I knew from seminary study. Pam had briefly been with a religious order in her early life and had intended on spending her life as a nun. As was often the case for intelligent independent women entering religious life, it was not celibacy or a vow of poverty that diverted her from the religious life, but rather a hard-driving Mother Superior to whom she was not about to render a vow of obedience. In the long run, I owe much to this mean-spirited Mother Superior!

Shortly after I turned 40, I had a sense it was time to seriously seek out a church home. My search was aided by attending a meeting of Parents and Friends of Lesbians and Gays, better known as PFLAG. I met some wonderful older straight couples who attended a local United Church of Christ and invited me to attend some Sunday. I was informed that the pastor of that church was open to having gay and lesbian members of his congregation who were not required to hide their sexual orientation from the rest of the membership. He had performed at least one gay union service for a lesbian couple at his church. I began attending that church and soon joined. With the help of Pam and ten others we formed the congregation's first gay and lesbian fellowship - Another Voice.

I remained in that congregation for four years but later left with Pam as we sought a form of worship more comfortable for her in the Episcopal Church. Often referred to euphemistically as "Catholic lite," we believed the Episcopal Church would be a nice compromise for us. The first Episcopal Church we visited was quite an experience. As newcomers, we were each greeted with roses as we signed the guest register. The following week we got a letter from the welcoming committee saying how nice it was to have us in the congregation and that they hoped we would be back the next Sunday. I responded to the letter with my own letter of thanks, and explained that "my partner, Pam, and I were happy to know there was such a friendly church nearby where we both could feel comfortable with the religious tradition."

Needless to say, there was no follow-up letter or telephone call from the welcoming committee. When we returned to that church the next Sunday, no one spoke to us. A couple years later we would learn from a closeted lesbian of that church that the woman who headed up the welcoming committee was very homophobic. Obviously when she got my letter, her mission to recruit us as members took on much less urgency.

Knowing that a spiritual fellowship would be important for the growth of our relationship, Pam and I kept searching for a church home. At her suggestion we tried another Episcopal Church in a less upscale neighborhood. Pam had attended a funeral at that church many years before and thought it might be worth exploring. I will always remember that hot August day we stepped foot inside St. Paul's and found a lovely, older church edifice, somewhat sparsely attended but full of love. It was a diverse congregation with African Americans, Latinos, Asians and Caucasians. The rector was a distinguished gentleman approaching 60 who we would later learn was gay and in a committed relationship with his partner of several years. The rector did not hide his gayness but did not shove it in people's faces either. The fact that his partner, Michael, was a very active member of the church was clearly accepted by the faithful, and anyone who was upset with this fact had long before left the congregation.

On this Sunday, the rector was explaining how the governing board of the church, the vestry, had decided to sell off some parcels of real property which had been left to the church. With the proceeds from the sale of this property, the congregation was going to form three outreach committees to Latinos, families, and gay and lesbian people to increase the church fold and do important ministry to these three surrounding communities. As I sat that morning contemplating my long journey for a church home, I gave thanks to God that I had been brought to a place where a church was willing to let go of wealth and invest in people. I gave thanks to God that I had been brought to a place where it really made no difference whether you were African American, Latino, Asian, or gay or straight, male or female, for you were welcome.

While I certainly enjoyed my thirteen years in this parish and was very active to the point of being secretary of vestry for a year, I confess the liturgical differences were a stretch for me coming from my humble United Methodist background. But I stuck with this congregation for 13 years as it proceeded through the trauma of having the American Episcopal church clashing with the larger worldwide Anglican Communion over issues of ordaining openly gay and lesbian individuals as rectors and bishops. Shortly after the wonderful rector who had greeted Pam and I that first Sunday retired, I chose to go back to the United Church of Christ, a more comfortable liturgical format for me. Pam admitted that "once a Catholic, always a Catholic," and that she was no longer interested in attending the Episcopal Church either.

And so, I admit to being a nomad when it comes to organized religion. I do not expect churches to be perfect, for we as human beings are not perfect, and, therefore, the institutions we support and grow reflect our imperfections. But when it comes to accepting human beings who were created to be gay or lesbian, I believe God has given the greater Christian church one of its mightiest tests of faith. The LGBT community has much of what the church needs - honesty about who we are. As was the common phrase thirty years ago, the LGBT community is giving the church a chance to "get real" about what it means to be open and accepting of all people, and what it means to be comfortable in your own skin so that you can accept differences without being threatened by those differences.

CHAPTER NINE

The Biblical Roots Of Homophobia

The question is frequently and fairly asked, "What are we to do with the Biblical texts condemning homosexual practice?" This question can only be answered by addressing what role the Holy Scriptures are to play in modern life and times. Of course fundamentalist Christians see the debate premised upon the authority of the scriptures to direct the appropriateness of all human behavior in the 21st century A.D. as it might have been in the 21st century B.C. This is what I call the "how do I know, the Bible tells me so," understanding of Christianity. To embrace the notion that the Bible, some of which was written in the cultural milieu of many centuries before Christ, no longer completely addresses the needs or concerns of the 21st century is to properly acknowledge that the scriptures should be symbolically embraced and not literally followed in every respect in 2010.

As Emmet Fox wrote in his book Diagrams for Living: "Well-meaning people have read the Bible day after day, year after year, until they almost know it by heart, and yet they have never touched the living thing at all. Most of the criticism leveled against the Bible by modern thinkers is solely due to the fact that they take the Bible literally, whereas Divine Providence meant it to be taken as parable."

The truth of the scriptures is that throughout all the writings of the prophets and the New Testament accounts of Christ's teachings, there is not one mention of homosexuality. Don't you suppose that if homosexuality was truly such an abomination so that gay people should be put to death, the prophets and Christ would have made some mention of it as an unholy practice? The truth of the scriptures is that the mention in Leviticus 20:13 of putting to death homosexuals was part of a larger holiness code which touched every aspect of life, including what foods to eat and clothes to wear and which also called for such extraordinarily harsh penalties such as death for children who spoke back to their parents. In an age where parents and child advocates understand that corporal punishment should be prohibited today, our society is not about to re-institute the practice of putting to death children who speak back to their parents!

The truth of the scriptures is that there are so many references to the appropriateness of slavery, particularly in the Old Testament, that if one were truly to be a follower of the literal word today, he or she would condone slavery! Those who know the history of our nation surely realize the Bible was once quoted to support the practice of slavery. No one wishes to return to those days. I don't think in any part of the civilized world today, we see slavery as anything else but an abomination to the human spirit and free will. Were any religious leader or church to call for the re-establishment of slavery in our society, there would be such an outrage and condemnation of those precepts that the story would be covered on CNN for months. Would not an enlightened reader of the scriptures conclude that just as we cannot condone slavery on the basis of Old Testament scriptures, so we should not condemn homosexuality by Biblical authority either? Leviticus 20:13 was written in an environment where the continuation of the Jewish race was a dire necessity and anything, such as homosexuality, which might have lessened procreation, was to be avoided.

There are millions of religious people, myself included, who believe God's wisdom is most certainly contained in much of what we call our Bible, but that these scriptures were nevertheless written by human beings who were susceptible to incorporating the cultural biases of their time into what they wrote. In other words, we do not believe that the Biblical authors were merely taking down God's dictation. To take this interpretation of the authority of the scriptures is not to throw the theological baby out with the bath water. Rather it is to recognize that the authors of the Bible were attempting to be faithful messengers of God's word just like each of us do each day who committed our lives to God's work. In their diligence to preach God's word through their writings, they nevertheless let their humanness and limited cultural perspective of the times show through.

This latter perspective on the authority of the scriptures in my life came to me long before I realized my true sexual orientation as lesbian. Indeed, I would never have entered the ministry if I had believed that all the verses of the New Testament prohibiting women from having a significant role in the church were divinely inspired. To interpret these Biblical pronouncements for "women to keep silent in the church," as God's word to modern man, would have been to deny the very call to the ministry I felt in 1971.

I understand the desire many hold to believe all the scriptures are infallible, concrete and decipherable. We all are searching for answers in a world that seems to provide only questions for the meaning of human existence. Yet, the essence of faith is in the living of the questions. Why do we need to have a pat theological answer for every question? We are not any more capable of understanding the Process of our Creation than a year old baby is capable of reading Moby Dick or understanding calculus.

Yet to hear most of the evangelical leaders of the day, you would clearly get the message that they know exactly what God had in mind when he created our world, and that gays and lesbians were certainly not a good part of that Creation. But their very scriptural underpinnings must be challenged for they are not consistent nor sound.

Let us be honest about it. There is not one individual in the Christian community who can truly claim to be a Biblical literalist. By this I mean an individual who subscribes to the belief that every word and concept of the Bible is applicable to life in the 21st century. This was best exemplified to me by a "700 Club" I watched a few years ago which naturally Pat Robertson was hosting. Let me be clear I do not frequently watch this show, but every now and then I will tune in to find out what my theological opposites are preaching now.

In this particular program, Robertson was answering some of his mail. One woman had written in to Pat asking him what was the appropriate way to "deal" with homosexuals. Pat responded with his usual "love the sinner but not the sin" philosophy, commenting that it was not for the Christian community to hate homosexuals, but at the same time, the Christian community had an obligation to strenuously oppose a practice that would result in an individual's loss of life to everlasting damnation, as the Bible had made it so clear would happen.

Pat's next letter came from a woman who cited to the New Testament scripture requiring women to have their heads covered whenever worshiping God. "What were women today to do, given this admonition?" The letter further inquired whether or not "women were violating God's laws if they didn't cover their heads in church."

Robertson responded with a little laugh that he knew he'd "probably get some letters over his answer about this," but that this admonition for women to cover their heads contained in the New Testament scriptures "was just something out of the culture of those times and not necessarily applicable to women today!" This 700 Club episode highlights the point that even the staunchest Biblical literalist uses the Bible at his convenience. Pat, if you claim the Bible is to be interpreted literally as to the admonition against homosexuality, why are you not taking seriously its admonition for women to cover their heads in worship? Are you not the one who is picking over the scriptures like a buffet supper to see what fits your tastes and what does not?

Why have so many individuals on the Religious Right particularly singled out homosexuality as the greatest threat to our nation's moral climate? The simple answer, well documented in Mel White's book *Stranger at the Gate* is that homophobia raises money. Stereotyping gays and lesbians as immoral, despicable and depraved individuals puts money in the Religious Right's coffers. One would wonder how much money Robertson, the late Jerry Falwell, James Dobson and countless other religious fundamentalists would have raised if they had started a major campaign against divorce! No doubt tens of thousands of their heterosexual followers have been divorced or victimized by divorce, and condemning this social problem would hit too close to home. Not much money would be sent in for the cause of ending divorce, the real threat to the institution of marriage.

It is easy to pick on a small minority group such as gays and lesbians, blaming them for much of the world's social ills, if you will never be a part of that minority, nor have a good friend or relative who is an LGBT person. It is easy to join the majority oppressors. Ignorance breeds prejudice and hatred to minority groups. This is certainly true of the enemies of LGBT people - they prefer to remain ignorant about our community and the basis for our sexual orientation. They refuse to acknowledge the possibility that we are a good part of God's creation, and that our living with a member of the same sex is not a "sexual preference" but a God given orientation.

As this book is being submitted to the publisher in March 2010, a disturbing example of the cruel and evil ways in which the religious right is stirring up hatred toward the LGBT community in Africa is coming through broadcasts on ABC news. Citing to the verses in the Bible previously discussed, and displaying pornographic materials of homosexual acts to large congregations of African Christian adult church members, white and African preachers are talking about the "homosexual agenda" to destroy marriage throughout the world. So much animosity has been stirred up against the LGBT community in Uganda, that most gay and lesbian people have gone into hiding, and those who remain out are in fear for their lives. Those who remain out have good reason for being in fear of their lives for legislation is being proposed in Uganda's legislature which would make the practice of homosexuality punishable by death.

The evangelical pastors, both white and African, who have created this furor and hatred are actual provoking genocide against the LGBT community. Will no one stop them? Does anyone other than ABC news want to give attention to this outrageous situation? Do we say as the United States of America we are more enlightened than "those people," and we would never allow this atrocity in America! Have we forgotten about the young gay male Matthew Shepard and his horrendous torture and murder in the Wyoming by Caucasian males within the last decade? Have we forgotten about the several transgender people who have been recently murdered in our country simply for being who they are? Have we forgotten that Hitler placed homosexual individuals on his most hated list and exterminated them with the same ferocity as six million Jews?

We all have a fundamental desire to judge other people, and to look down our nose at someone we consider less moral or normal than ourselves. Because gays and lesbians will always constitute a small minority of the population, they can expect a fight for understanding and acceptance forever.

In sum, this author believes that the Biblical verses condemning homosexuality came out of a cultural bias which would condemn any practice counter-productive to the continuation of the Jewish community. People coupling up with the same sex would not serve the purpose of the procreation of that race. The very survival of the race was at stake and every man and woman capable of producing children were called upon to fulfill this mission. When they could not do so, particularly the barren women were pitied and made to feel less than a woman. Is this still where we find ourselves on this overcrowded planet in the late 21st century? I think not.

You will often hear opponents of gay and lesbian marriage argue that it is more than apparent the Creator intended unions between men and women for the express purpose of procreation. Therefore, marriage should be exclusively reserved to the heterosexual community. But if this is true, why do we permit marriage between senior citizens, or to any heterosexuals who are incapable or do not wish to create children? Should we not require a declaration of intent to have children before issuing marriage licenses if this is the primary reason for Holy Matrimony?

The agonizing and offensive attempt by some Christians of a fundamentalist persuasion to understand how gay individuals figure into the Christian Church was very recently demonstrated to me during a luncheon I had with someone whom I once considered a pastoral friend. This pastor called me out of the blue one day and wanted to have lunch. I had preached a year before at his independent, interdenominational but largely African American parish during "herstory" month about my experiences as a woman pastor in the early years of the 1970's.

My "friend" knew I was a lesbian from the first time we met when he saw a picture of my partner on my chamber's desk and asked who she was. He met with me that day because he had heard I was the new supervising judge of the delinquency courts in his district and that we both had the common desire to start some programs for African American boys to keep them from delinquency.

Now a year later we were sitting in an upscale restaurant he had chosen for lunch discussing his money woes of his fledgling church. It was quite clear he was seeking my financial support for his church. Halfway through lunch I point blank asked him, "How do you and your membership regard gay and lesbian people?" He looked astonished and with wide eyes replied, "Well, we treat them no differently and welcome them to our midst the same as we would drug addicts."

I sat for a moment and just stared at him. I finally conveyed my feelings that I did not quite agree to the comparison of gay people with drug addicts and alcoholics. Those individuals should not be condemned for their disease but that a sexual orientation other than heterosexual was not a disease but a God given trait. He never replied but I am sure to this day he never quite understood how his response was unloving or offensive. Perhaps later when he pondered why I did not give him any money for his church, he might have figured out why I refrained from doing so.

CHAPTER TEN

Where Do We Go From Here?

As we enter the second decade of the 21st century, it is quite apparent that for many years to come, we will live through a period of time as many commentators have observed when the gay rights movement will take two steps forward, and one step back. This can be seen in the not so insignificant legal victories by the gay community which have occurred here and there, only to be followed by some disheartening reminder of American society's homophobia. This struggle forward, only to be pushed back, is best exemplified with what happened in my home state of California concerning the issue of same-sex marriage.

After the California Supreme Court took what many considered at the time to be a very brave initial stand for gay rights in May 2008 by ruling that the denial of marriage to gay and lesbian individuals was an abridgement of equal protection, the monied forces of Christian fundamentalism came sweeping into the state with the introduction of Proposition 8, an initiative to be voted on by the people in the November 2008 election, which would amend the California constitution to make only marriage between a man and woman legal. The Mormon Church as well as the Knights of Columbus, to name but two such organizations, outspent the anti-Proposition 8 forces mightily, and waged a vicious television and radio campaign on the evils of same sex marriage. By a narrow margin of 52 percent to 48 percent, Proposition 8 passed, outlawing same sex marriage in California.

Many were astounded by this turn of events not understanding how President Obama could be swept into office on the same date that Proposition 8 passed. Unfortunately the demographics revealed that many of the minority populations who voted for President Obama also voted to eliminate same sex marriage in California. Ironic, isn't it? Even more disconcerting was the fact that when the California Supreme Court had to take up the issue of Proposition 8's constitutionality, all but one justice ruled that the initiative process of the people could be used to amend our constitution, resulting in the denial for gays and lesbians of the right to marry. Somehow within the space of a year, equal protection for gays and lesbians to marry their partners had magically disappeared!

Chief Justice Ronald George who first authored the opinion to allow same-sex marriage in May 2008 and then a year later voted to uphold the ban on gay marriage encompassed in Proposition 8, has lectured about the state decrying the unencumbered effect of the initiative process in California. Of course, this does not cure the denial of equal protection for gays and lesbians to marry.

One bright spot in all this California madness over same sex marriage is that there was a window of opportunity for 18,000 of us gay and lesbian couples to get married between June 2008 and the November election in 2008. This was the period from June 2008 when the Supreme Court said initially we should not be denied the right to marry to the November 2008 election when the California electorate voted for Proposition 8 outlawing the practice in November 2008 by an initiative which amended our constitution. I not only had the privilege as a jurist of performing two of these weddings myself, but my partner and I availed ourselves of the same opportunity on July 7, 2008, in the Beverly Hills Courthouse performed by a dear woman jurist who was more than happy to give legal permanency to gay and lesbian committed relationships. Although a very small affair, my partner and I realized we were making history that afternoon.

When the constitutionality of Proposition 8 was before the California Supreme Court in 2009, the justices at least recognized they could not make Proposition 8's applicability retroactive to the marriages they had authorized earlier. They concluded that gay and lesbian couples had relied upon the law as established by them earlier in their May 2008 ruling that same sex marriage should be extended to the gay community through the basis of equal protection. Proposition 8 had not yet been passed at this time, so these marriages should stand. Now we have this crazy result in California where 18,000 same sex couples are married, but the privilege will evermore be denied to other gay and lesbian couples. If ever there was a denial of equal protection to the gay and lesbian community, it surely exists now where one segment of the community is legally married, but those who want to follow in our footsteps as gay and lesbian people will be denied the privilege. This is the ticking legal time bomb that will no doubt come back to haunt the anti-gay forces. As younger heterosexual people more readily accept gay and lesbian people as no less normal or deserving than themselves, they will join the forces who shout "how can this injustice and inequality remain?"

As this book is being written, the federal district court trial on the constitutionality of Proposition 8 is being heard. Curiously, Ted Olson, a former Solicitor General to the United States Supreme Court under a Republican Presidency, has chosen to represent gay and lesbian people in their fight for same sex marriage, clearly noting that this is just an issue of fundamental fairness and equality under the law. If he gets it, why can't other conservative individuals get it? Wasn't the Republican Party once about having government stay out of an individual's life as much as possible, while the Democratic party represented policies for the greater common good? Somehow through the decades one party has morphed into a moral authoritarian figure exclaiming that traditional marriage between a man and a woman is the common good, while the other party has held to a less than prophetic role in developing unworkable policies like "don't ask, don't tell," in a weak attempt to give gays and lesbians some civil rights recognition and privacy.

As one who has taught a law school course in Religion and the Law, it appears to me that many well-meaning people do not grasp the incredible abridgement happening to the concept of the separation of church and state in the gay marriage debate. Those who have read the Constitution or at least heard about it from high school civics should remember that the first part of the First Amendment states that "Congress shall make no law respecting an establishment of religion, or prohibiting the free exercise thereof." Allowing religious individuals and institutions to establish and impose upon the nation their religious idea of a proper marriage as one between a man and a woman is nothing more than a violation of the first clause of the First Amendment. Marriage as a civil institution representing a binding contract between two people should remain a legal concept. Every religious organization, under the free exercise clause of the First Amendment, should retain the right to deny marriage to gay and lesbian people. Such religious organizations can issue additional certificates of marriage which confirm that this couple's union was sanctified by their church.

If everyone would agree throughout the United States that all such contracts which we know today as marriage heretofore be designated as civil unions, whether they take place between a man and a woman or two lesbian or gay two individuals, this would leave theologically conservative churches free to perform services and issue marriage certificates for heterosexual couples only. When and if this occurs, the gay marriage issue evaporates as matter of state.

The issue of same sex marriage is just one of the civil rights concerns that faces our community. In fact, in the early years as this issue surfacied, some in the gay and lesbian community decried the fact that this issue of the right to marry was being given top priority while many states continued to deny basic human rights against discrimination in housing, employment and education. I would have no argument with those who say undoing the "Don't Ask, Don't Tell" policy of the military is an en essential gay rights issue which must be addressed with vigor.

On March 28, 2010, the program CBS Sunday Morning, reporter Kimberly Dozier reported the said story of two lesbian women soldiers who had been honorably discharged from the military under this policy of "Don't ask, Don' Tell." On March 25, 2010, Defense Secretary Robert Gates announced that he would be proposing new military regulations which could slow or virtually stop expulsion of gays such as these two women soldiers of distinction. Sgt. Lacey Presley was a medic who under dangerous conditions had saved reporter Dozier's life as well as the lives of others on the front lines of Iraq at the time. For this valor, Sgt. Presley was awarded the Bronze Star.

Sgt. Presley was in love with another military woman Holly Thompson. It came to Sgt. Presley's attention that one of her superior officers was using drugs and she reported it to his superior officer. In retaliation for her report of this drug use, pictures of her kissing Holly Thompson surfaced and an investigation of her sexual orientation began. Before all was said and done, this long time military woman who had hoped to make the military her career, was honorably discharged for this conduct. Sgt. Presley had never been overt about her behavior in any way, nor had her partner. It is only one's guess who was sneaking about in her private life. The bottom line is that the military lost one outstanding soldier over the issue of whom she chose to love.

Representative Patrick Murphy, the first Iraq veteran to serve in the United States House of Representatives is doing all he can to reverse the "Don't Ask, Don't Tell" policy which has continued to cause the persecution of gay military personnel. As Rep. Murphy points out it has cost 1.3 billion to throw out these gay and lesbian soldiers over these years at a time our nation needs every available soldier to fight on two war fronts. The "Don't Ask, Don't Tell" policy was a backroom deal with the military in 1993 fashioned by the Clinton administration to try and end discrimination against gays in the military. As stated above, the policy seemed to only make matters worse, with the military stepping up the attempt to wander into people's private lives and discriminate against those who are not heterosexual.

Several nations allow gays to serve openly in the military. Great Britian, as well as our neighbor to the north, Canada, allows gays to serve openly. Israel.has for years allowed for service by gays and lesbians. One gay major in the Israeli army stated in the CBS report, as far as the Israeli army is concerned, "you can tell, but we don't care." He went on to relate that his long time companion often visited him at military installations, that the men and women of his company liked and accepted his partner with qualms. If one of the finest armies in the world had adopted this policy of openness and acceptance of gays and lesbians in the military, what is wrong with us?

The same sex marriage issue has perhaps become the predominate issue of our time because it involves the right of gay and lesbian people to form meaningful intimate relationships which also embraces the right to freedom of association and privacy. It is from this right to marry that the gay and lesbian community can build stability in their families, and be given the economic opportunities to buffer those families.

This latter concern of economic rights for gay and lesbian partners and families is no better exemplified than in my own personal circumstance. For federal taxation purposes, my spouse and I are denied thousands of dollars in tax exemptions because we cannot legally marry. While California's Domestic Partnership law gives us the same state tax benefits as heterosexually married people, this is not so for federal taxes. I am the main bread earner in my family, since my partner is fully disabled and has nothing other then her social security disability benefits. I cannot claim her as a dependent on my federal return, I will never have access to her social security benefits even though she worked for over 35 years prior to her disability. For the past two years, when it comes time to file our taxes, we file a joint state return which Turbo Tax instructs us to create a "fictitious federal return" to be filed with our state return only. This is due to the fact that California state taxation is based upon all the information contained in the federal form, particularly Schedule A information, and in order for the state franchise taxing authority to assess our tax liability appropriately, we need to appear as a married couple. In this process, I learned I would have received an additional $6,000 back on my federal taxes last year if I could have claimed my partner. In short, there is no truth to the rumor that Domestic Partnership laws overcome the inequity created by a denial of same sex marriage.

While we need to understand that the full recognition of civil rights for gays and lesbians may take some time to evolve, we should never give up hope that it will happen. It took the African American community over 60 years to move from the twisted "separate but equal" mindset of our United States Supreme Court in the 1890's, to the Brown v. Board of

Education decision in 1954 which outlawed segregation. When viewed historically, our gay rights movement is still relatively young. As more and more people of influence and political import courageously choose to reveal their gay or lesbian identity, the majority will finally conclude our community is truly just another minority group, deserving of basic human rights such as the right to marry, be left alone, to be free from employment and housing discrimination. Whether the larger Christian church decides to promote these civil rights for us remains to be seen. Indeed, this is a defining moment for Christians who truly follow the life and teachings of Christ, our Lord and Savior, who never condemned us once in all this teachings.

In the meantime, we need to hold on to the truth that God loves us and affirms us as we are. We need to create our own spiritual support groups if the larger Christian Church is unwilling to have us in its midst. We need to continue to educate others about what it means to be gay or lesbian. And for those who are hiding in the closet, afraid that they will lose some status, wealth or recognition by coming out, it is your moment to decide if you can continue to deny the integrity of your soul. It is time for you to ask yourself, "could it be that by coming out to the world I could do the one thing God put me on this earth to do so that others may not suffer from discrimination and hatred?" I am not for publically outing people who wish to remain in the closet. I see coming out as a matter of personal choice. God will continue to love you even if you do not come out, and I recognize it is easier for some people to come out than others. What I can tell you from my own life is that not hiding your sexual orientation and embracing the full person God created you to be is the most freeing experience you will every have. As St. Paul observed nearly two thousand years ago for followers of Christ, "if God is for us, who can be against us?"

About The Author

After graduating from Syracuse University in 1972 with a Bachelor of Arts degree in political science, Martha E. Bellinger attended Princeton Theological Seminary's Master of Divinity program from 1972 to 1974, and was graduated from Boston University School of Theology in 1975 with a Master of Theology degree. She was ordained in the United Methodist Church in 1974 and after her graduation from Boston University, served as pastor for two small parishes in Upstate New York.

During her seminary years, Reverend Bellinger recognized her sexual orientation was lesbian and she met her first partner at Princeton. Being separated from her partner, remaining thoroughly in the closet yet facing discrimination as the first woman pastor in her district of the church, Rev. Bellinger decided to change directions in life and eventually traveled to California with this partner to attend Whittier College School of Law from which she earned a Juris Doctorate in 1982.

After spending some time in the Los Angeles County District Attorney's office as a deputy district attorney, she joined the Los Angeles Superior Court bench in 1991. Judge Bellinger also served as an adjunct professor of law at La Verne University College of Law from 1988 to 1996, and has plans to rejoin that faculty in the spring semester of 2011, teaching Religion and the Law.

Judge Bellinger was legally married to her spouse, Pam, on July 7, 2008. They live in Claremont California, where Judge Bellinger belongs to the United Church of Christ, an open and affirming congregation to the LGBT community.